SACRED WRITINGS BY WOMEN IN MEDICINE

PENELOPE APPLEGARTH, MSN, FNP-C, FCN

WITH CONTRIBUTIONS FROM:

Surani Hayre-Kwan DNP, FNP

Shari Kovner, MSN, FNP

Maria Pacheco, MSN, FNP

Chris Perkowsa, PA

Jennifer Shipp, MSN, FNP

Mary Wyman, MSN, FNP

BALBOA.PRESS

A DIVISION OF HAY HOUSE

Balboa Press books may be ordered through booksellers or by contacting:

Balboa Press
A Division of Hay House
1663 Liberty Drive
Bloomington, IN 47403
www.balboapress.com
844-682-1282

Print information available on the last page.

ISBN: 978-1-9822-7636-2 (sc)
ISBN: 978-1-9822-7638-6 (hc)
ISBN: 978-1-9822-7637-9 (e)

Library of Congress Control Number: 2021922122

Balboa Press rev. date: 12/09/2021

Sacred: *connected with God (or the gods)*
Merriam-Webster Dictionary

"...heal thyself"
The Holy Bible *(Luke 4:23)*

Contents

Acknowledgements

I want to thank my colleagues that contributed to making this book by adding their rich and personal writings. The purpose of the book is to share this process that has contributed to each of our personal growth. The shared writings are but a sample of the depth of our personal stories and by bringing them to consciousness and sharing parts of ourselves, and being heard without judgment has allowed us the freedom needed to build greater resiliency in our lives.

I want to thank Lea Knight, artist, for her design for the book cover and adding drawings for the pages to give more texture and interesting images in the book.

I thank Jeanne House, herself an author, for her guidance, wisdom, and experience, in helping me navigate the publishing process. Her guidance was essential in getting this book into print. Her experience with marketing and book promotion has been such a gift to this novice.

I am grateful for Hay House's Writer Workshops. Their offering to writers is a very valuable asset for writers. I am grateful to Balboa Press, the self-publishing arm of Hay House, that allows a new author to self-publish their work.

My thanks to Andreanna Zobian Mason for her editing skills and suggestions. I believe her recommendation have made this book an interesting read for anyone picking it up.

Introduction

The beginning of a once-in-a-lifetime pandemic seemed like a good time to take on this project. Being home more with limited places to go, allowed for more free time than I ever remember having in my life. The content I wanted to share for this book had already been written; each contributor selected what they would share. This was not a simple task! We had so many writings to choose from over the years, each rich and meaningful to us and the feeling of uncertainty that these writings would be as meaningful to others.

The purpose for writing this book is to share the experience that has become a deep and rich part of my personal and professional life. The coming together of a small group of women who share the same professional career of medicine, and practiced in the same community health system, along with the many frustrations and challenges and the joys and heart-warming intimacy of caring for others has bonded us in ways none of us could have imagined. We have become close in our sisterhood of shared experiences; a shared intimacy and connection developed between all of us. My hope in writing this book is to inspire others to reach out to their professional colleagues in a similar manner; to promote comradery and intimacy that helps sustain and build resiliency in one's professional life.

This is not an original idea or concept. Rachel Naomi Remen, MD, wrote at least two books on the need for story telling as a means for resilience and healing. Her first book was titled "Kitchen Table Wisdom: Stories That Heal", offered this idea of shared healing through the stories of our lives and work. Sharing stories from our life experiences helps deepen connection and understanding of our own character, our values, our wounds, our healing, and the threads of meaning that bind us to one another in our humanity.

We started out as a small group of women seeking a way to express ourselves. We did not want our expression to be one of complaining about the frustrations of working in healthcare at a time of limited resources and productivity targets, but as an expression of who we are and why we are drawn to continue to work in healthcare. We chose to use the model of "Kitchen Table Wisdom" and coming together once a month, using narrative writing around our experiences. The idea was to build relationships and support for one another as we developed an outlet to honor our values and ideals that inspired us as healthcare providers.

Our gatherings soon evolved into something more meaningful for all of us and became more than an expression of our work- we began to write about what was happening within our families, our communities and the world. We added structure by selecting a new word every month- to provide focus in our writings. We collectively have a wealth of feelings and history, coloring our perceptions of experience in our careers and personal lives. We were not doing therapy; we were building resilience with our ideals and avoiding the negative feelings of cynicism. We picked a word each month to reflect on during the coming weeks. The word could relate to our experience as providers, such as, "compassion", "fear", "change" or something more abstract, like "being", "justice" or "mercy". The monthly reflection served to help us maintain awareness on what we do and feel as clinicians.

The monthly ritual that evolved for our meetings was to gather at the home of one of our members who cooked the meal. We would then eat a meal that often reflected the monthly word. Many times, some of us would come late, directly from work, grateful for a nourishing meal with friends. At the table we talk, laugh, share news of our families, work, and feelings. Our camaraderie deepened over the years and often lifted our mood that had been challenged through patient concerns or life events. Our meetings provided a circle of support that has helped to validate our humanness and build resiliency for the wearing effects of healthcare that can lead to burnout for providers.

Our evening meal is one of such special significance of nurturing and nourishment. Mary has often spent as much time selecting our amazing meals as we have reflecting on the monthly word. The group may bring some side dishes, like a salad or other complement and we all tend to contribute to desert (chocolate is an important ingredient for healing and health in our circle!). The meals are an important part of the experience and feel like a gift to each of us; we cannot thank Mary enough for her loving touch.

Following our shared meal, we move to the living room and sit together in silent meditation for 5 minutes as we center ourselves. One person has emerged as our "wordsmith". She considers the selected word and brings a poem or passage that embodies a meaningful connection with that word. A copy of the poem/passage is shared with everyone present and read silently. Two or three volunteers to read the poem/passage out loud, using their voice to interpret the words. We share the words that stand out for us and create meaningful imagery.

We then use a prompt based on the monthly word and begin to write. The goal is to write from our personal experiences or feelings what arise around the monthly word prompt. Writing typically lasts about 10 minutes and then we read aloud to the group. There is no judgement from the group, advice or even comments; we let the writings resonate within us. Through this process, we offer support of each other and acceptance of our humanness and of our experiences.

At the close of our evening, we choose our word for the next month, often sparked by national events or local clinic changes. We close our time together with another 5-minute meditation.

We have been meeting for more than nine years now. Members have come and gone, and some returned. Life changes experienced within the group have been life-altering; marriage, divorce, becoming mothers and grandparents, experiencing death of loved ones, completion of doctorate degrees, and job changes. It is with joy that we plan to continue in our circle of support.

In creating this book, I asked each of the members wishing to contribute to write a short biography about themselves. I wanted them to include what brought them to the group and other details they wished to share about their background, their careers, and their lives. Not all those that attend the monthly group meeting chose to contribute to the book for many different reasons. These contributions are a rich sampling from our nine-year journey together. I have included the menus and poetry/passage selections from the dates chosen by the contributors when available. There will be some that have not been included, as over time we have misplaced or not written down all the details for each contribution chosen in this collection. The writings from each contributor are as they were written in the moment and have not been edited. Grammar, punctuation, and syntax may not meet literary expertise. We felt it was important to share what was written and how it was written in the moment. It is our hope that this content will bring to others a practice that can add to your work, your life, and your sustainability with your work.

CHAPTER 1

Integration

Integration

Definition of Integration from Merriam-Webster Dictionary

1. The action or process of integrating
2. The intermixing of people or groups previously segregated
3. The finding of an integral or integrals in mathematic
4. The coordination of processes in the nervous system, including diverse sensory information and motor impulses
5. The process by which a well-balanced psyche becomes whole as the developing ego organizes the id, and the state that results or that treatment seeks to create or restore by countering the fragmenting effect of defense mechanism

In healing terms, we talk a lot about "wholeness", a balance of the physical, mental, emotional, and spiritual aspects of ourselves. To achieve this "wholeness" requires a deep assessment of what we know of ourselves and what we are not aware of. The conscious self and the unconscious self. To examine the unconscious requires being willing to look. One way of looking can be through writing as done in the group exercise of having a word and a prompt and allowing what comes to mind to be expressed without fear of criticism or judgement. As from my experience and from others in this group, often we were surprised by the story in our lives that would surface. We often recalled beautiful, heartfelt experiences, as well as painful, emotional experiences.

Our lives are so busy and so full of distractions, it is often hard to find time or take the time for reflection on an event or a single day. We rush through what must be done and often then shut off when we are not needed to be present to our work, our relationships, or our menial tasks. If we do not set time aside for ourselves to reflect, we do not have an opportunity to get to know who we are, what makes us happy, sad, scared, anxious, depressed, joyful or impassioned. And if we do not have a safe outlet to share the ups and downs of ourselves, we do not learn to integrate the wholeness of ourselves. For it is through deep listening and sharing and feeling heard that we can change. We can learn to accept all of our flaws, our fears and loathing as part of who we are without criticism of ourselves but with acceptance.

How many times have you reacted to a situation or a comment and later felt embarrassed or regret from your reaction? How many times have you asked yourself the question, "Where did that come from?", "Why do I get so defensive when people say or do (fill in the blank)?" or "Why did I say this or that when that is not how I feel or felt?".

Medicine is defined in the Merriam-Webster dictionary as:

1. a: substance or preparation used in treating disease
    b: something that affects well-being

2. a: the science and art dealing with the maintenance of health and the prevention, alleviation, or cure of disease
    b: the branch of medicine concerned with the nonsurgical treatment of disease

3. a substance (such as a drug or potion) used to treat something other than disease, an object held in traditional American Indian belief to give control over natural or magical forces

Through the years of working as a practitioner, patient's report that medicine can occur in the medical office when they feel "heard", "witnessed", "validated" and "listened to". New research is showing that a patient's pain can be reduced when they feel their practitioner was compassionate towards them. Several books have been written about this and shown this can also be a cost saving not only for the patients but also to the health care system. Compassion is a perception by the patient and takes less than a minute from the practitioner to express through their attentive presence with the patient.

Compassion is something all peoples need to feel accepted and validated.

Integration is a personal journey to reach a sense of wholeness that affects all of life experience. Without allowing for the comfortable and uncomfortable parts of ourselves to be integrated into the whole of ourselves we are vulnerable to work burnout as a care provider, as well as not achieving a sense of being in control at the highest level of our lives' expressions. To achieve integration requires first compassion towards ourselves. This is not something taught in our culture, this practice has not been valued, or promoted until recently in literature and through research of the benefits of compassionate selfcare. It does require emotional work, reflection, and allowing for time in our day for selfcare. These actions take a commitment for setting aside time each day. This time is not given to us, but must be sought out as a desire, a plan for our own wellbeing and health maintenance. The benefits can be liberating and provide a deeper foundation for interpersonal relationships as well as health benefits. To be at peace with oneself reduces anxiety, improves sleep and has proven to lower blood pressure, and improve blood sugar levels in diabetics.

Through the experience of the past 9 years, this group of medical practitioners, have fostered this environment of compassion and validation through sharing our writings, experiencing being heard without judgement or fear of criticism. We have all expressed the importance of the group itself for holding us during our difficult times and celebrating our times of achievement and victories. This is not a typical support group. We have no leader outside our "word smith" that allows for direction through words for our writings. We are equal participants in this journey of self-reflection and discovery. Because of the high value we place on the participation of this process we wanted to share it with others. Our shared hope is that others may find a circle of others that are interested in writing and sharing their own stories in a safe environment and find the richness we have been able to find and share with one another.

We feel it is good medicine and a stabilizing practice that builds resilience.

Chapter 2

The Women Contributors

Jenny's Bio

After working as a nurse practitioner for 25 years, I fell in love with narrative medicine. It taught me a new way of listening and attending to the stories of my patients. Several colleagues were interested in forming a group so we could listen to each other. I brought the idea of bringing a poem and prompt for a spontaneous writing exercise. Mary offered to make us dinner and meet at her lovely home once a month. It is the perfect combination of friendship, good food, and deep sharing that fills me and nourishes my love for my sister practitioners and the work we do, caring for our patients.

[Jen is our words smith. I am adding to her biography as she was humble in her introduction. She has touched so many lives in her 25 years of nursing and Nurse Practitioner work. Her calm presence has been the foundation of our group and one of the reasons we still are meeting. Following our shared meal, Jenny leads us in a 5-minute silent meditation, she sounds the chime to start and to pull us back together. She holds us together through the ritual of our meeting and with her amazing ability to find poems that speak to the word chosen for each meeting. The poems she finds are so intriguing and sets the atmosphere for the prompt she uses to direct our writing. She has a real gift in doing this and I am so thankful for her literary breath of knowledge.

Before we start our writing from the poem and prompt, Jenny gives us the meaning and history of the word we have chosen for the meeting. We choose a word that act as the theme for the month at the close of the meeting the month prior. We are educated on the depth of word's meaning as used over time, the historical and cultural origin, and ways the meaning of the word has evolved over time. The understanding of the word lends to the choice of the poem for the evening. This ritual adds depth and a deeper look into ways to write from our experiences in relation to the word, the poem, and the prompt she sets for us. Jenny is the glue that holds the structure for our meetings.]

Mary's Bio

I was born in a little corn town in Ohio. Our large Irish Catholic family moved to a Chicago suburb where I did most of my "growing up". My sister and I were the only girls in a sea of boys. The idea of becoming a nurse wasn't in my consciousness until I had my daughter on The Farm in Tennessee. There, I experienced the incredible support of strong women midwives and the sacredness of birth. I applied to nursing school with the goal of becoming a midwife myself. As life would have it, I have assisted many, many more in leaving this world, than entering it. As of today, I have been in Nursing for 40 years! It has offered such a front row seat to humanity. The breadth and depth of what I have witnessed and participated in has been an immense honor; has been so rich and full of lessons, joys, sorrows, so many options and choices. I have worked in hospitals, home care, public health, international health, and now college health. One period that stretched me the most was the ten years during the AIDS crisis. Home infusion therapy, I worked with an incredibly dedicated and innovative team- easing the dying process for many. I have been cracked wide open and yet kept showing up. Sometimes, so fearful and other times crazy courageous.

While working as a Nurse Practitioner at a FQHC, again surrounded by heroes, several of us learned about Rachel Remen and Narrative medicine. I took one of Rachel Remen's classes. Jenny and I decided to start this group that would help to support our process as primary care Nurse Practitioners.

So, we began. One month, then the next month. Each month, there was some fine tuning. Since the meetings are mostly at my house, I became the cook. Initially, it was very basic food. I would put things in the crock pot in the morning in hopes it would be edible when we all arrived at dinner time for our group. But, as time went on, I saw how our group was evolving to feed us on many levels- healthy, yummy food; always dessert; check in and support; meditating; a reading; our writings to a prompt; closing. This group morphed into a lifeline- a means for all of us to see the beauty and power that we embodied.

So we kept coming back- for 9 years.

It is now truly a sacred healing circle.

Surani's Bio

The first gathering came as an invitation for dinner, to meet, share patient care triumphs and despairs- together. The idea was loosely based on work Jenny had done on reflection, compassion and healthcare providers responding to burnout.

I wasn't sure I would be able to come frequently. My two teenage girls were still at home, work was busy and life was HECTIC. But I decided that the company was worth my effort, so I showed up, not sure what to expect.

What happened was magic- even in the first evening. I still remember the poem we read together. It reminded me of the space where I grew up, in the country, with the sense of endless sky and beauty. The feeling of sharing our experiences, our feelings and how they affected us in the moment was intensely powerful. I felt supported by this group of women, sharing similar experiences in our clinical environments. We were all different ages but our thoughts together seemed to have a timeless quality- almost as if we were part of a huge, long story of human caring.

When I left that first meeting, I had this incredible sense of power, like I was overflowing with energy. I was so glad I decided to give myself this time to recover in partnership.

Healing words.

Introduce the essence of each of us.
What matters in our lives?

Penelope Applegarth, MSN, FNP-C, FCN

What drew us to participate with our monthly
gatherings for these past 9 years?

What keeps us gathering together monthly?

What drew us to medicine/ healthcare, to
begin with and what keeps us in it?

I am a first-generation Indian on my father's side, multiple generations on my mother's. I love being a nurse and cherish my patients' trust. I have a passion for science, and the truth and mysteries it continues to reveal.

I attended the first gathering for our organization nurse practitioners because I liked all of the women and rarely got time to see them. The idea of having dinner together, with time to talk, was very appealing. I was not sure what to expect but felt like it was a safe space to explore.

I had done reflective writing many years ago, but never with consistency and never beyond the borders of my own experiences. What I was unprepared for was how much I would learn about the impact of events on our lives. Sometimes the smallest things are recalled with incredible clarity and continue to reverberate in our minds and soul for years. Taking these out to reflect on with a prompt and witnesses can be like therapy- for all of us.

We started with the idea that the host would provide the main dish, and we would bring accompaniments to the meal, including something delicious for dessert; this evolved into the host cooking the entire meal and all of us arriving exhausted and hungry after work. Dessert could be fancy chocolate, seasonal fruit, or ice cream—sometimes we had all at the same time. The time we spend around the table is just as healing as that with pen and paper. We share updates from our lives in the past month, changes in work, decisions about the future, and connections with our shared past.

Shari's Bio

How I ended up here?

I still have in some drawer an old index card that says: I am going to be a doctor – Shari age 12. So, I guess my journey started there. I was fascinated with medicine – I read books about doctors treating needy people all over the world and that's what I wanted to do. I wanted to take care of people. I liked reading about the history of medicine and how are bodies worked. I wanted to be a helper. I also was fascinated by different cultures, ancient traditions, and exotic places, and I loved animals and nature stories.

I loved science but fell in with the social science crowd- and became an anthropology major until one of my anthropology professors, who was from the Miwok tribe told me that his people hated anthropologists because they never did anything for the people they studied. So… back to the try sciences and I fell in love again with biology, anatomy, and physiology. And started thinking about going to Nursing school. At the time I had this new type of medical provider called a nurse practitioner. She worked at Planned Parenthood. She felt like a hero to me- smart, caring, competent, and so kind.

To get into the nursing program at UCSF, I had to get some experience as a nurse – so far I was working as a vet assistance and needed some humans to learn about- back to the county clinic and off to Nursing School. I liked working with children and adolescents, and I was afraid of how I would handle emergencies so I ended up taking a special rotation at Highland hospital in Oakland- a very eye- opening experience but I found out I loved ER work, and I also took a special class through the medical school on teaching puberty and sex education in the schools.

Thus, I developed a lifelong love of teaching adolescents about their bodies and eventually taking care their health.

After nursing school, I worked 4-5 years as an Emergency Room nurse, I loved the work but was ready to get to into NP school – I went to Davis FNP program and through a friend was able to do an internship in Tuba City Arizona on the Navajo reservation at the referral hospital – One of the most fascinating, experiences of my life. I felt like I was in my own adventure movie, with non-stop learning combining my love of anthropology with medicine.

When I returned to California, I got a job with the Public Health Service and helped set up a clinic at Hamilton Air Force base for the newly arriving, sometimes very sick, Indochinese refugees. The clinic was staffed by 2 NP's.

When that clinic closed, I started working at Russian River Health Center (RRHC) – it was the beginning of the AID's epidemic, I worked with brilliant doctors and was learning constantly, and my husband and I wanted a family.

I ended up working at RRHC and Occidental Health Centers (part of the same community health system) for many years -mostly part time so I would be with my kids, I continued to teach SEX ED in their classrooms which my own kids had to survive. But boy we can talk about anything in our house. I worked in the newly formed

Teen Clinic from the time it has existed. How lucky I am to live so many of my dreams, to work with the same kind and competent medical providers that I have always been inspired by and now to sit with, laugh, share, eat, meditate, and write with my lovely colleagues.

Penny's Bio

I joined this group of exceptional women healers in 2011. I had the honor of working for an organization that created several rural health clinics where I first met these women. I was teaching nursing as a full-time instructor at the local junior college in their associate degree RN program. I was feeling a need to continue to work in health care as a Nurse Practitioner along with teaching. I applied for a position with the organization and I was hired as a locum provider, filling in when needed for other providers. As it turned out, I was able to do this work at least one evening shift a week along with my full-time teaching. I was so grateful.

I have had the privilege of working in health care for close to 50 years. Yes, if you do the math, I am retirement age. I did retire from teaching and found I still have much to give as a Nurse Practitioner. I am working 24 hours a week and it is fabulous. I am so grateful I can continue caring for patients at the same Rural Clinic and grateful for the part time schedule.

As a child I had envisioned myself as a physician. Life led me to my current profession as a Nurse Practitioner and I am so pleased that this is my career. Life events has led me on a variety of medical career paths prior to my becoming a nurse practitioner. At the age of 18, I went to a technical college for Dental Assisting and worked in this capacity for 5 years as I completed a bachelor's degree in Social Welfare with a second degree in Criminology, emphasis on Juvenile Corrections. (Long story on this path that I will not go into here. It had to do with being young and not doing well in chemistry and I had to do well to get into the RN program). I then went to work for a private psychiatric in-patient hospital. I worked with adolescents, many of them were in this facility to avoid Juvenile Hall for first time offenders as well as several teens with very wealthy parents that had multiple convictions, usually around illicit drugs. It did not take long working with this organization to awaken in me my desire to practice medicine in some capacity. I enrolled in a Psychiatric Technician Program and completed this license. I then enrolled in an associate degree RN program and completed it. (I now had enough maturity to do well in Chemistry!) I worked as an RN in the psychiatric hospital with adolescents and adults full time. I also worked 2 shifts a week in the local district hospital on the Medical -Surgical unit to further develop my skills as an RN. I loved both areas of work.

In the late 1980's, reimbursement for private psychiatric care was practically dissolved. My work with adolescents at the private psychiatric hospital allowed us to have the patients for the amount of time needed to help them adjust to the changes in their life, to deal with their childhood traumas and learn effective coping skills that would allow them to have a functional productive life. Following the change in insurance practices the length of stay was reduce to 30 days. Thirty days had been the standard time needed for a thorough assessment period and care plan development of goals for their hospitalization. The standard of care was now altered to meet reimbursement allowances and the type of long-term care that had been the gold standard now gone. I decided then to pursue advancing my career on the medical side. I took a job working full time in a level one trauma center. I worked in their remarkably busy ICU unit and I loved it. I learned so much on the job and sought out continuing education like a sponge. After 3 years working in the ICU, I decided I wanted to pursue a Master's in Nursing and complete the Nurse Practitioner program. I graduated in this capacity in 1994 and have enjoyed every day of this career. I feel it is a privilege and an honor to care for others in this capacity, as I did as an RN prior. The remarkable connection and intimacy of care and concern that is felt and shared in a patient office visit is a gift, a richness, that feeds my belief that people are innately good and enjoy this recognition of who they are. Often, this connection can open the gateway toward healing.

My mental health background has taught me the importance of the need for self-emotional health and balance. Our monthly meetings are a perfect mix of comradery, creativity, emotional release and sharing with a group of women bonded by our common care and concern for others, through our careers and in our personal lives. In monthly meetings we can expose ourselves, the areas of wounding, the areas of generous strength, resilience, and the deep connection in our lives. There is not "judgement" in our circle, just compassion, listening, and being present to one another. Such a gift.

Through the years of our meetings, the uniqueness of our circle, with the personal growth and support our meetings provide us, the desire to want to share this model of participation to others, especially those working in health care evolved. Health care by its very nature can be both emotionally and physically consuming. Being able to have a monthly outlet that isn't judgmental, doesn't question and allows the freedom to express what needs to be expressed has provided a healing that none of us had known was needed.

Maria's Bio

I was born in Peru. My family moved to California four months before my fourth birthday. English was difficult for me and my father prohibited us from speaking Spanish. We needed to blend in. Ah yes, the old "melting pot". We were good "Americans" and much of our culture melted away or became unrecognizable.

Language – I remember being astounded by the vocabulary and comprehension of my children between the ages of three and four. There is so much going on in those young brains. Learning to express emotions, problem solving, patience, imagination and much more. For me, language was different. I was confused and learned English by watching television. Not by watching educational programs on PBS but by watching I Love Lucy and The Andy Griffith Show. I understood quite a bit but when I went to kindergarten, I struggled. I remember the teacher shouting and pointing her finger at me as I peacefully looked at a book in the "Cozy Corner". I didn't last long with her and had to repeat kindergarten. The second time it was more pleasant. Miss Lee was an angel and helped me in so many ways.

Communicating has always mystified me. I dreaded public speaking and struggled in grad school with all the papers culminating in my master's thesis. I think that's what they called it. See, even now the words are not always perfect.

When I was asked to join the writing group, I was nervous. I saw the women in the group as intelligent, professional, powerful women. A little intimidating and I wondered if I would fit in.

Was this going to be another melting pot experiment? Did I have anything left to melt? All these worries melted away after my first meeting. The women were kind, loving and accepting. I felt blessed!

In this group, I am able to connect with a side of myself that had been hidden even from me. When I write, I just write, the words rise up from somewhere deep, deep inside me. I am just as amazed by my writings as everyone else. I love our group and the connections we have developed. It's like therapy but more fun. I learn so much about myself. The painful experiences from my past that I had buried in secret spots are magically exhumed and shared. Healing happens before my eyes. The weight is lifted and there is a shift which I cannot put to words.

Chris's Bio

I graduated as a Physician Assistant in 1990. Then became a Nurse Midwife in 1998. I might as well have become an MD, but I chose not to after agonizing a lot about that. I am a healer, and mostly I am working with women. This is where I have arrived after 30 years of working in the medical field.

I have worked in many settings—in and out of hospital, very rural clinics in New Mexico, a stint in a county hospital in the Bronx on the OB/GYN team, part of my midwifery training in Cuba, and worked on the Mexican border in birth centers. I've taken time off to birth and raise my baby with special needs, to renovate an adobe house in NM, to work part time and enjoy life apart from work. I've always seemed to bridge two worlds in my career, with herbs and hanging out with radical midwives; as well as working with federal clinics most of my career; strongly believing they are the closest things we have to socialized medicine in this crazy country.

The last decade I stopped attending births and retooled my career with the study of Ayurvedic constitutional medicine and gained more hands-on skills offering Belly focused massage for women. As part of an Integrative medicine clinic, I inherited a women's writing group over 6 years ago, from Jenny Shipp, who is a part of this book. She mentored me into the ways of Writing as Medicine. I thoroughly enjoy facilitating this amazing group weekly in a Group Medical Visit.

Over the past 5 years it has been an honor to attend my own writing group with these amazing Medicine Women in this book, eat the best meals, converse, share, meditate and write together. The best part is listening to each other's words and stories: True Nourishment!

Chapter 3

Words, Prompts, Poems, Recipes, and Writings

03/11/2014

Word: Anger

Defined in Merriam-Webster:
1. a strong felling of displeasure and usually of antagonism
2. a threatening or violent appearance of state: RAGE

Poem: From "Report from the Field" by Dorothea Tanning (1919-2012)

"Only the artist will be held responsible
For something so far unsaid but true,
For having the crust to let the hysterical
Earnest of genuine feeling show through",

Meal: Irish vegetarian stew with stout ale and seitan, Fresh bread, Green salad; Desserts

Prompt: Describe a day when you experienced anger.
By Penny

It was one of "those days"!!!

I am already an hour plus behind on my patient schedule. I had a patient emergency. She had been so dehydrated with vomiting and diarrhea for the past 3 days. She was a woman in her mid-50s, appeared frail and weak. I was thinking "possible norovirus". She was refusing to go to the emergency department, she wanted IV fluids and something to stop her vomiting. We could provide these measures in the clinic.

We gave her a liter of normal saline by IV and Zofran for her nausea and vomiting. She was still vomiting and having diarrhea. After another hour of encouraging her, she finally agreed to go to the hospital's emergency department. She had a ride with her and I called the emergency room to let them know she was coming.

My next patient is very angry that she had to wait for over an hour to be seen and she was letting me know that she was unhappy! She then pulled out a list of all her medications she needed refilled. Then she produced a page of all her medical complaints. She proceeded to give me a detailed, complete history behind each of her physical complaints: she has nail fungus for the past 3 years and "no one has helped with curing it". She has chronic back pain and wants to go on medical disability because she cannot do her work with this much pain. She wants a referral to a dermatologist to look at her skin because she does not trust General Practitioners. And on and on and on....

[I want to leave the room and go Home!]

I smile and ask her which items on her list are the most important to address today? I tell her I that I want to help and will and ask if we can do this in stages? Her anger does not lessen. I let her know I can do the referral and medication refills following the visit and assure her it will be done later today. Her disability request requires her to bring in the appropriate paperwork from the State and can be done without her present if she fills out her part of the form.

I am now so far behind patients are asking to be rescheduled.

09/22/2020

Word: Apocalypse

Merriam-Webster defines this word as:

1. (a) One of the Jewish and Christian writings of 200 B.C. to
   A. D. 150 marked by pseudonymity, symbolic imagery,
   and the expectation of an imminent cosmic cataclysm in
   which God destroys the ruling powers of evil and raises the
   righteous to life in a messianic kingdom
   (b) capitalized: REVELATION
2. (a) something viewed as prophetic revelation
   (b) ARMAGEDDON
3. (a) a large, disastrous fire: INFERNO
   (b) a great disaster

Poem: O Taste And See by Denise Levertov (born 10/24/1923, died
12/20 1997)
"The world is not with us enough. O taste and see"

Meal: To Go: Jam Joy Noodle Bowls and 3 forms of chocolate for
dessert. Location: in my back yard! Spaced out. First time we have
seen each other in person since 3/2020.

Prompt: Write about a time you had a revelation.
By Mary

Now. Many revelations right now. This is the first time we are
together in person since a minuscule virus changed life for the whole
world. This reveals a huge revelation! Control? We truly have so little
real control.

But also, right now, the word apocalypse-which was so appropriately chosen for this time actually has a deeper meaning. Something not as obvious. Jenny says "it isn't fire and brimstone but rather about uncovering or revealing all kinds of mysteries". Wow, looking at apocalypse that way is quite liberating. And, yes, so many intricacies have been revealed over the last challenging and fear filled 6 months.

Revelations - how much we genuinely need each other, on a cellular level. How I feel like crying right now because I get to see these wonderful faces- that I love.

Revelation - how much time I spend not in the present moment.

Revelation - how this moment, right now, is so over the top profound that it is hard to use words. I am seeing the sweetness of the presence of all of us. We are each jewels in our own right- and when we fit together-whoa- it is marvelous, mosaic masterpiece!

Revelation - I am missing much of the fruit of this life- worrying-planning, problem solving (isn't this what nurses do well?) Right now- be here in this precious moment. Coming to my "senses".

I see there is so much fruit available to me. So much to taste, see, feel. The abject beauty of dusk, the greyish purple sky that is darkening around us, the subtle sound of a few crickets. I am seeing the change. Evening, the promise of softening edges, the coolness of air on my skin.

I have no past story to write tonight as tonight is the story. This band of amazing women. Look at what we have created. A bond that now feels so natural, so solid, with connecting fibers that run from heads and hearts.

The delight of getting to see each other, knowing that we have each been traversing this wild time, this roller coaster of extremes, in our own ways. AND we are doing it. And we are here, now.

Having a plague rage, somehow doesn't matter tonight. We are laughing, and comparing some harsh stories, but mostly we are steeped in the sweetness, the joy and deep security in being together. And we are freeing the word Apocalypse. We are uncovering, revealing the deeper truth of the absolute miraculous and beauty of each other---which is always helped by a side of chocolate.

01/14/2014

Word: Aware

Defined in Merriam-Webster as:
1. Having or showing realization, perception, or knowledge
2. Archaic: WATCHFUL, WARY

Poem: (not archived)

Meal: North African Tagine (with dates, yam, garbanzo in tomato and coconut with couscous, broccoli and mushrooms); beautiful dessert

Recipe for North African Tagine: (The above additional ingredients were added to this traditional recipe and the flavors were amazing.)

2 tablespoons olive oil
½ teaspoon turmeric
3 teaspoons ground cumin
1 teaspoon paprika
¼ cup finely chopped cilantro
½ cup finely chopped flat-leaf parsley
2 cloves garlic, minced
1 (14 ounce) can diced tomatoes, undrained
1 large fennel bulb, cut into ½ inch wedges
1 ¼ pounds Yukon Gold potatoes, peeled and cut into 6 wedges
2 cups chopped peeled turnips
4 carrots, cut in half lengthwise and then into 3-inch sticks
1 cup vegetable broth
1 cup frozen baby peas

2 tablespoons fresh lemon juice
Fresh cilantro sprigs

INSTRUCTIONS:

Heat oil in a large skillet over medium heat. Add turmeric, cumin, and paprika, cook, stirring, until the spices begin to foam.

Add cilantro, parsley, garlic, and tomatoes, cook, stirring until they're well blended. Add fennel, potatoes, turnips, carrots, and broth. Then reduce heat to medium. Cover tightly and cook until potatoes and carrots are tender (about 30 minutes).

Add peas and cook until they are thoroughly heated. Season the mixture with salt, pepper, and lemon juice.

Prompt: Describe becoming aware of a healing moment...
By Penny

I am in counseling describing my impressions of the last years of my marriage, of how I had felt I had given up trying to make things better for him-as nothing seemed to help or be enough. His negativity, aloofness, long silences, were incomprehensible to me. Yet, I had no intention of bringing our life together to an end. I was living my life, doing the work I loved, found peace in other things.

And now felt so broken-so empty, that I was being discarded for "I know not why?" This ending opened up the deepest wounds of my soul.

My counselor says, "Could it be that this rejection was not about who you are-but about who he is?"

Light bulbs turned on, "Oh my". Reminding me of my own narcissism. Wow. I had to look again, over and over. What is mine to carry and what is his. Redefining, reframing, rebuilding myself. New eyes, new awareness. Healing moments. Healing work is lifelong!

01/24/2017

Word: Beginning

Defined in Merriam Webster as:
1. The point at which something begins: start
2. the first part
3. Origin, source

Poem: "The Banishment" (from Paradise Lost) by John Milton (1608-1674)

So spake our mother Eve, and Adam heard
well pleased, but answered not: for now too nigh
the Archangel stood, and from the other hill
to their fixed station, all in bright array
the Cherubim descended: on the ground
gliding meteorous, as evening mist
risen from the river o'er the marish glides,
and gathers ground fast at the labourer's heel
homeward returning. High in front advanced,
the brandished sword of God before them blazed
fierce as a comet; which with torrid heat,
and vapour as the Lybyan air adjust,
began to parch that temperate clime; where at
in either hand the hastening Angel caught
our lingering parents, and to the eastern gate
led them direct, and down the cliff as fast
to the subjected plain; then disappeared.
They, looking back, all the eastern side beheld

of Paradise, so late their happy seat,
waved over by that flaming brand, the gate
with dreadful faces thronged and fiery arms.
Some natural tears they dropped, but wiped them soon,
the world was all before them, where to choose
their place of rest, and Providence their guide:
They hand in hand with wandering steps and slow,
through Eden took their solitary way.

Meal: Asian noodles with tofu, veggies, salad, bread, Ho-Ho chocolate

Prompt: Write about what helped you begin again?
By Surani

The sun helped me begin again.
The days continued to occur- sun-up, sun rise, beautiful sky.
An opportunity for a new start- a fresh start.
And the sun cycled through the day- the shadows moving across the room, the yard and finally the sun setting in the west headed to the other side of the planet and beginning a new day.
The air helped me begin again.
Crisp, clean, invigorating.
Breathing in. Breathing out.
It is not time for me to die- my body wants to stay alive.
So my lungs process the air, oxygen pulled through alveoli, lifted by my blood and offered all
over my body like a gift.
People helped me begin again.
Surrounded by humans,

busy with the work of life.

Driving, walking, biking.

Working in offices, teaching, opening stores.

Life continues no matter what.

And it continues through birth and death and birth again.

I felt the power of being human, alive and made it through each day

grateful for the ability to live

even without trying.

12/11/2018

Word: Being

Defined in Merriam Webster:
1. (a) the quality or state of having existence
    (b) 1-something that is conceivable and hence capable of existing
       2- something that actually exists
       3- the totality of existing things
    (c) conscious existence: LIFE
2. the qualities that constitute an existent thing: ESSENCE
3. a living thing, especially: PERSON

Poem: "Hag Riding" by Lucille Clifton (1936-2010)

"...galloping down the highway of my life
something hopeful rises in me
rises and runs me out into the road
and i lob my fierce thigh high
over the rump of the day and honey
i ride i ride"

Meal: Fried eggplant, tahini, veggie Shepard's pie, green beans; Blue berries, chocolate, meringue

Recipe for Vegan Shepard's Pie
1 ½ pound russet potatoes, peeled and quartered
6 tablespoons vegan butter, divided
1 cup of parsnips, diced
1 medium onion, chopped
1 cup carrots, diced

3 cloves of garlic, minced

1 cup frozen corn

1 cup frozen peas

1 cup vegetable broth

1 tablespoon tomato paste

1 teaspoon Worcestershire sauce

2 teaspoons fresh rosemary

1 teaspoon fresh thyme

1 cup cooked lentils

¼ cup plant-based milk

INSTRUCTIONS:

Pre-heat oven to 400 degrees F.

Place the potatoes in a large pot and cover with cold water and sprinkle in one teaspoon salt. Bring the water to a boil, reduce to simmer, and cook until potatoes are fork tender (approximately 20 minutes).

In a large skillet melt 2 tablespoons of the butter over medium heat. Add in the onion, parsnips, and carrots and sauté for 8 minutes or until the onions are translucent.

Stir in the garlic and cook for an additional minute.

Add in the corn, peas, rosemary, thyme, Worcestershire sauce, vegetable broth and tomato paste and stir to combine. Gently fold in the cooked lentils. Take off the heat. If baking the pie in a separate dish, place the mixture in the baking dish.

Once the potatoes are done, drain and add into a large bowl with 4 tablespoons of butter. Mash the potatoes until creamy and few small chunks remain. Stir in the milk and season with salt and pepper.

Arrange the mashed potatoes on top of the vegetable mixture. Using a fork, rough up the potatoes a bit so there are soft peaks. Bake in the oven for 30 minutes and until the potatoes have started to brown slightly.

Garnish with fresh herbs if desire.

Prompt: "A time when you experienced your fierce self…"
By Penny

My fierce self emerges whenever I am told I couldn't do something because I was a girl, later a woman. These words would put me into the strongest force of defiance I know, and I was on a mission to prove these words wrong.

It was a stance from early childhood, having been born a "girl", labeled by my father as 'good for nothing', will never amount to anything, useless." Wow. What a rage that would stir up in me.

Then the father of my children first said I could go to college once he graduated (as I had worked full time for him to be able to complete his degree). Then it was I could go to college after we had children as we didn't want to be old like my parents and have no energy for our children. My parents had me at ages 35 (my mother) and 45 (my father) and I had 2 younger sisters. My parents were always too tired and moody, unhappy.

Then two sons later it was my time for college, and I was told "no", I should wait until the boys are in school. I said "No, I can go part time. It's MY time." He couldn't stand it, I was getting straight A's and I was happy.

Now fiercely fighting to be "good for something" as I was doing something I felt called to do, gain a career doing something to help others and I loved science.

Our fighting grew to be more and more, soon we were done fighting and the marriage was over.

Fiercely I moved forward, finishing one degree and then another and another.

Just don't tell me "I can't do something because I am a woman...." I cherish every cell of this womanhood fiercely!!!

Prompt: Write about a time you experienced your fierce self
By Chris

At the foot of the bed, the edge of the pool, in the pool, on the table, between her thighs "push, breathe, stop bleeding, start, stop, breathe, push, breathe…!"

I remember one woman in the tub laboring; all she could do was talk over and over about the mythical picnic they were on to get through each contraction; she'd say a line, I'd repeat it back to her—over and over. The people, the food, the place, walking, playing, over and over for hours we shouted out the "picnic" together.

Another woman in deep labor asking if she is going to die? Right in my face she asked. I said "no" with fierce certainty. I knew she was transitioning to birth…A woman seizing as the baby slid out of her; barking orders.

A woman bleeding so much blood—barking orders to keep her alive and on this side. Another woman, with whom I failed to fend off the doctors who wanted her to have an episiotomy. I stood up to them, stayed my ground between her legs saying, "look the baby is coming—no necessita!!" They pushed me aside and cut her without anesthesia with dull scissors (this was in Cuba in 1998).

Another woman, 8 cm, bag of waters intact, but not progressing no matter what we did most of the night. I sent her home from the birth center to her own home to rest in her own bed…at 8 cm…. She did deliver the next day on the next shift. I had to be fierce when I signed out to the next midwife, who questioned my management.

44

Fierce—call the ambulance, she is aborting!

Fierce—jump onto the boat taxi (in Maine), pull on gloves and catch the baby right there. Then transport to the birth center to recover. Fierce—poor mommasita of 4; didn't want the 5th stopped labor at 8 cm also (Texas border). Put her in bathtub, fed her dinner, let her sleep all night. Back on shift in the morning; time to have the baby you don't want mommasita; let's do some nipple stimulation to get your contractions going again and let the baby come.

Myself as a midwife, Fierce. Good to remember that side of myself, good to remember some of the women, all Fierce themselves.

8-11-2014

Word: Breath

Defined in Merriam Webster:
1. (a) air filled with a fragrance or odor
   (b) a slight indication: SUGGESTION
2. (a) the faculty of breathing
   (b) an act of breathing
   (c) opportunity or time to breathe: RESPITE
3. a slight breeze
4. (a) air inhaled and exhaled in breathing
   (b) something produced by breath or breathing (such as moisture on a cold surface) 5. a spoken sound: UTTERANCE
6. SPIRIT, ANIMATION

Poem: Taken from "The Moment Again" by William Stafford (1914-1993)

"In breath, where kingdoms hide,
one little turn at the end
is king, again, again, again.
That moment hides in the breath
to be time's king: others may vaunt;
that one will never pretend."

Meal: Sautéed vegetables and couscous, green salad, lots of dessert & multi-berry crisp

Writing Prompt: A moment when you were aware of the kingdom in your breath
By Surani

It happens when I run.
The breath is like a battle at first.
Burning.
Forcing its way in and out
Telling me to slow down, go slower
Walk,
Catch my breath
But I ignore it.
Or I acknowledge it but continue to push on.
I am controlling the breath then- focused on the in and out
Telling my other self that this will pass.

And then I forget.

It is like it is effortless.

Something you forget about because it is so smooth and easy.

Like a smooth ride on silk

Without pressure to force it harder

or slow it down

And then I am always amazed at how easy it is- I rule the little piece

of world I occupy

My kingdom.

11/20/2019

Word: Chafing

Defined in Merriam Webster:
1. IRRITATE, VEX
2. To warm by rubbing especially with the hands
3. (a) to rub so as to wear away: ABRADE
    (b) to make sore by or as if by rubbing
4. To feel irritation, discontent, or impatience: FRET
5. a state of vexation: RAGE
6. injury or wear caused by friction

Poem: Taken from "The Critics" by Theodore Spencer (1902-1949)
"With difficulty the ship was built,
Launched with more difficulty still;
The cradle was a rotten one,
The harbor had clogged up with silt—
And then the barnacles fastened on."

Meal: Gado gado; Chocolate cake, ice cream

Prompt: Write about the barnacles.
By Maria

Barnacles
Grasping on to what is near
They don't concern themselves with appearances
Strength or EGO
They know they are at the bottom of the list
Not appreciated for their efforts

Not valued in society
Yet here they are
They arrive
They attach themselves to items considered worthless
They accept those items as they are
No judgement
Let us be here
With you
Become part of you
We see you
And are not afraid or threatened
By you
Your words
Your dirty looks
Your judgements
We are here attached to
You
We make you stronger
As you strengthen us
We are one
A team
We are equal
And together we are stronger
Than apart
I wonder how the barnacles know where to go
I ask them as I sit in the boat
Wondering if we'll sink
Silence
Water slapping the side of the boat

Water turning into words
"We feel the pain of the critics" they whisper
"we know they are crying for their past:
"We feel the broken cradle
And know we can make it strong again
We become the shell for the boat"
Smooth travels and shared travels
Together
We are stronger

09/08/2014

Word: Change

Defined in Merriam Webster:
1. (a) to make different in some particular: ALTER
    (b) to make radically different: TRANSFORM
    (c) to give a different position, course, or direction
2. (a) to replace with another
    (b) to make a shift from one to another: SWITCH
    (c) to exchange for an equivalent sum of money (as in smaller denominations or in a foreign currency)
    (d) to undergo a modification of
    (e) to put fresh clothes or covering on

Poem: selection from "Trying to Name What Doesn't Change" by Naomi Shihab Nye (born: 1952) taken from *Words Under the Words: Selected Poems (Portland, Oregon: Far Corner Book, 1995)*
"Peter isn't sure. He saw an abandoned track
near Sabinas, Mexico, and says a track without a train
is a changed track. The metal wasn't shiny anymore.
The wood was split and some of the ties were gone".

Meal: Shrimp, lemongrass, coconut milk with turmeric rice and limes; Green salad with beets and apples; chocolate and melon

TURMERIC Rice Recipe:
2 teaspoons olive oil
¼ Cup diced onion
½ teaspoon curry poser

1 teaspoon ground turmeric

2 cups chicken or vegetable broth

1 cup jasmine rice kosher salt

INSTRUCTIONS:

Heat medium sized pot with lid on stove top. Add oil and onion, heat until onion is tender, about 3 minutes. Add turmeric and curry powder and stir to heat and distribute for 15-30 seconds. Add broth and bring to a boil, add rice. Reduce heat to a simmer. Cover pot and cook for 20 minutes, covered the entire time. Remove from heat, fluff with a fork and add salt to taste before serving.

COCONUT MILK-LEMONGRASS SHRIMP RECIPE:

1 can (14 oz) coconut milk

2 stalks lemongrass, about 4-6" each, ends trimmed, coarsely chopped

1 large shallot, coarsely chopped

3 cloves of garlic

2 thick slices fresh ginger, peeled

2 tablespoons Sriracha

Zest and juice of 2 limes

25-30 large shrimp, peeled and deveined

1 Tablespoon extra-virgin olive oil

½ pound snow peas

INSTRUCTIONS:

Place coconut milk, lemongrass, shallot. Garlic, ginger, Sriracha, zest and lime juice in a blender. Puree until smooth. Reserve 1-1/4 cup of this liquid. In a large bowl, pour the rest of the coconut puree over the shrimp and let marinate for at least 3 hours in the refrigerator.

Heat olive oil over medium-high heat. Add snow peas and sauté for about 2 minutes. Add reserved coconut puree and let it cook for about one minute and let the liquid bubble. Add shrimp and sauté until cooked and opaque looking, about 3-4 minutes. Serve with the Turmeric Rice.

Prompt: A moment when you weren't sure….
By Jenny

My first Con. My first burned out, wouldn't touch meth again if you paid me, tattooed, tired, saw the world with you can't surprise me no matter what, eyes. A Con.

Pain in every part of his broken body. I gave him every pain med there was in the early days. What did I know? I learned that is just what we do. And so, I did and he was a hunched, toothless wreck who finally went back to prison for 2 years—I never asked why—but he came back and I had changed. I was doing narrative medicine and knew there was another way to meet my patients and so I did meet him. I looked and sat up and listened and saw him. And, I think he saw me see him. And we were changed.

And he is one of the men in my life. I have so few and in the clinic my life is filled with them and we saw each other and in the last year—spontaneously—He'd say, "OK, baby girl, I hear you, I hear you, I can live with it..." And I was startled and then understood. We had met and gave in and stood back and there was a respect and an intimacy based on time and trust and our changing selves. I felt seen. He was seen and there we were. An honor, witnessing one another.

5/17/2016

Word: Color

(Means at its origin to "cover" or "hide")

Defined in Merriam Webster:

1. (a) a phenomenon of light (such as red, brown, pink, or
       gray) or visual perception that enables one to differentiate
       otherwise identical objects

    (b) 1- the aspect of the appearance of objects and light sources
       that may be described in terms of hue, lightness, and
       saturation) for objects and hue, brightness, and saturation
       for light sources.

       2- a color other than and as contrasted with black, white,
       or gray

    (c) colors plural: clothing of a bright color: clothing that is
       neither dark nor light in color

2. something used to give color: PIGMENT

3. (a) two or more hues employed in a medium of presentation

    (b) the use or combination of colors

4. skin pigmentation other than epically darker than what is
    considered characteristic of people typically defined as white

5. complexion tint: BLUSH 6. to give color to

6. to change

    (a) influence

    (b) misrepresent, distort

    (c) gloss, excuse

7. characterize, label

Poem: (Not archived)

Meal: Biryani, yogurt, chutney; Cupcakes

Recipe for Biryani:

3 tablespoons olive oil or ghee

1 yellow onion cut into ½-inch cubes

1 tablespoon garlic minced

1 tablespoon ginger minced

1 Roma tomato minced finely

½ cup water

½ cup peas

1 carrot sliced into thin coins

2 russet potatoes peeled and chopped

1 green bell pepper sliced

2 stalks celery thinly sliced

1 cup cauliflower florets

2 teaspoons Kosher salt

¼ teaspoon cayenne pepper

½ teaspoon black pepper

2 teaspoon black pepper

2 teaspoons garam masala

1 teaspoon coriander

½ teaspoon ground turmeric

1 teaspoon cumin

½ teaspoon cinnamon

4 cups vegetable broth

2 cups basmati rice rinsed and drained

INSTRUCTIONS:

Add olive oil in a large Dutch oven over medium-high heat.

Add the onion, and cook until translucent, about 3-4 minutes.

Stir in garlic, ginger, tomatoes, and ½ cup water.

Bring to a simmer, and cook until the water has evaporated, about 10 minutes.

Add in the peas, carrot, potato, bell pepper, celery and cauliflower and stir well.

Add in the salt, cayenne, black pepper, garam masala, turmeric, cuin and cinnamon, stirring well.

Add in the vegetable broth and bring to a boil.

Rinse basmati rice.

Add in the basmati rice, reduce to low heat and cook (covered) for 18-20 minutes.

Turn off the heat and let sit, covered, for 5 minutes before opening and serving.

Prompt: Write about a time when you were surprised by what was under the covering
By Chris

Well, this has to be when I met my daughter Emmalina, as she was born out of the cover of my body. Being pregnant is one thing. Giving birth is another. Being a mother is a whole other thing, far and away a whole other thing.

Meeting you first with your quiet movements within me, then your heartbeat over doppler, then seeing you in dreams. Then, those last weeks trying so hard to connect and talk you into turning from breech position.

The day we went to turn you, you kicked out your water bag—such excitement! You were coming somehow—either breech or by C Section, I had no idea at that point, but it was clear with broken waters you were coming very soon. Labor in breech, labor, labor, it was long but not too strong and they let me labor without cutting me!!! Finally at the end you sped up and then, first touch as you crowned— "a girl!!", then much tumble, squawk—this little, little being!

I hadn't seen your eyes yet, but your hand—I saw your hand, the crease, such surprise, such knowing all at once: Oh, so this is who is here, this is why that and that. Oh, now I understand, I get it, I get everything and my floppy little China girl there she was, and she has Down Syndrome. I was so surprised and elated and not sure all at the same time…!

This was a surprise-all of a sudden my life turns a hard right, and I have no idea what will unfold, but I knew: I am a mother, a fierce advocate, who licks her baby head of crusted birth juices—so naturally and primal. I know this girl is mine to place in my pouch until she comes all together—like a kangaroo baby, needing lots more time to form and adapt. Just stay on my chest and breast for hours and days; as long as it takes…you will emerge, and you are so well.

12 years later you have emerged so well, you live, you thrive. I am still so surprised it was you who came out from the cover of me.

10/17/2017

Word: Dress

Merriam Webster defines as:
1. (a) to make or set straight
   (b) to arrange in a straight line and at proper intervals (troops, equipment, etc.)
2. to prepare for use or service
3. to add decorative details or accessories to: EMBELLISH
4. (a) to put clothes on
   (b) to provide with clothing
5. archaic: DRESS DOWN
6. (a) to apply dressings or medicaments to

Poem: Selection from "Solitude" by Tomas Transtromer
"The head lights of the oncoming car
bore down on me as I wrestled the wheel through a slick
of terror, clear and slippery as egg-whites.
The seconds grew and grew—
making more room for me—
stretching huge as hospitals."

Meal: Mexican food, Green salad; Apple pie, Chocolate ice cream, pistachio ice cream, Spanish Turron Alemandra

Prompt: Write about a moment when the millions in your heart became one.
By Chris

My friend said it takes a tragedy like this to remember we all love each other, we really do love each other. And you lost your house, your mother, your father—they incinerated on the spot—cremated in their driveway with no time to escape. I heard the father's hip prosthesis melted to the car door handle and that is how he was identified. I melted there too. (Tubbs fire October 9, 2017) Or how about the time we were practically alone on the beach in Maine, kayaking, riding in the surf on our boats. Once we landed, I turned on my phone and joined the millions: "ping, ping, ping, ping, ping" in came the voice messages, and as I listened the story unfolded. I looked to the south sky, towards New York, and I felt the world in motion, all eyes on the TV screens and the skies. I joined in and was one of the millions aware of the tragedy, the outrageous tragedy, blowing up like the fires this week. Where will they strike next; pop, pop, pop another plume of smoke goes up.

Why do I not feel it like this, viscerally, when there is a slaughter in Syria, or Afghanistan or Niger, or the Congo, or Vietnam, Tibet, Myanmar, Nepal? I am so white, so American, and now so Californian. But the threat of terror nearby catapults me out of my solitude, my small world, my isolation, and I am right there with the millions of people, the ones I, of course, love so much.

07/18/2017

Word: Floating

Defined in Merriam Webster:
1. Buoyed on or in a fluid
2. Located out of the normal position
   (a) continually drifting or changing position
   (b) not presently committed or invested
   (c) short-term and usually not funded (d) having no fixed value or rate

Poem: Taken from "Pantoum of the Great Depression" by Donald Justice

"Our lives avoided tragedy
Simply by going on and on,
Without end and with little apparent meaning.
Oh, there were storms and small catastrophes."

Meal: Taco bar- soft and hard shell, cabbage salad; Key Lime cake, Frozen Caramel yogurt

Recipe for Shiitake Taco "Meat":
1 tablespoon extra-virgin olive oil
8 ounces shiitake mushrooms, stemmed and diced
1 cup crushed walnuts
1 tablespoon tamari
1 teaspoon chili powder
½ teaspoon balsamic vinegar
Sea salt and freshly ground black pepper

INSTRUCTIONS:

In a medium skillet, heat the olive oil over medium heat Add the mushrooms and cook, stirring only occasionally, until they begin to brown and soften, 3-4 minutes. Stir in the walnuts and lightly toast for 1-2 minutes. Stir in the tamari and the chili power. Add the balsamic vinegar and stir again. Remove from the heat and season with salt and pepper to taste.

Prompt: Write about the floating world and the real world
By Mary

She is floating, in the floating world. But she is not afraid. In fact, she seems to sit in such love; simple, no fuss, pure love. And she goes on and on.

It wasn't like this when she was first diagnosed. She had that look of a trapped animal. She was suffering, we were all suffering, because it was so hard to see those trapped animal eyes; to fully see the palpable sense of total helplessness. Her words, when I asked her if she was scared "mostly sad because there is nothing we can do, it will only get worse".

And she goes on and on. It has been 9 years since the Alzheimer's diagnosis. She has very few words left. Why is there so much love/ light/ comfort/ sense of the true world and true meaning in that house. Isn't this how "the real world" should feel?

The paint is chipping, the very cute but neurotic dog is peeing on the rugs in every room, the light bulbs burn out and my dad doesn't notice because there is much light from another source. Grace. They still totally love each. She knows she is cared for. She is absolutely buoyed and sustained by the care that comes back to her- because of her love. And she goes on and on.

So many people are touched by them, mom and dad. They've made it 68 years together. He still lovingly calls her Barbara Louisa. Her eyes still sparkle when he does. He has learned how to ask – just about anyone- for help. He now needs a day timer to keep track of the volunteers. Kathleen, lovely California granddaughter moves to Chicago, has been set to wonder and tears "they are so amazing". She unabashedly jumps in to care for her grandma.

When I left there last Sunday, I saw how she is mostly in the floating world versus the "real" world. When I said "I love you Mom" not thinking it would land, she sent back an arrow of love when she replied "I know"

Prompt: Write about the floating world and the real world....
By Maria

Entering her home
there is a stillness
She has been withdrawing for some time now
occasionally eating
throwing a smile at me
with her eyes wide open
sometimes a word or two
a memory we shared...
Between us love was palpable
We did not need words
we knew
Love had always been present
since she birthed me
There is a shift now
less of her presence
She had been singing songs
to comfort the children
her children
there had been an urgency in her voice
She NEEDED to sing
to still them
Now she is still
no words
small movements
eyes closed as she grips my hand with unexpected
STRENGTH

Something is missing
Time passes
There is less and less of her
And more and more of me
until I am left
with myself
and her memories
I miss you
Mamita Linda

11/18/2014

Word: Fluid

Defined in Merriam Webster:
1. (a) having particles that easily move and change their relative
    position without a separation of the mass and that easily
    yield to pressure: capable of flowing
    (b) subject to change or movement
2. characterized by or employing a smooth easy style
3. (a) available for various uses
    (b) LIQUID
4. a substance (such as a liquid or gas) tending to flow or conform
    to the outline of its container

Poem: From "To a Snake" by Jeffrey Harrison

"...*Now I*

am the who is ashamed, unable
to untangle my feelings,
braided into my DNA or buried
deep in the part of my brain
that is most like yours."

Meal: Soup with beets, sweet potatoes, beans, raised bread, spinach
ricotta, two salads; chocolate cake, berry tart

Prompt: Write about a river in my life.

By Penny

I feel my life is the "river". At times I float, I swim, I tread water, I sink and nearly drown. I guess I will be a dried riverbed at the end of life. Or my river may merge with the Sea in the end. Either way, I feel my life is ever moving and changing like the river. I love the imagery of it.

I feel like there is a fluidness to my being, a freeness of being, a power of energy, that at times barely can be contained by the riverbanks. Much of the time there is this gentleness of flow that is my life- moving along in time. Sometimes the movement is joyful, sometimes sad, sometimes rushing, sometimes gentle, sometimes fierce, and sometimes slow. Never stagnant. Always dynamic.

The "river" is the earthly elements that contain me and may define me. There is also an awareness of an energy that comes from within that interacts with the earthly elements, giving meaning and form to both my "life river" and an awareness that resides within that gives meaning and value to this life experience.

04/21/14

Word: HOME

Defined in Merriam Webster:
1. The place (such as a house or apartment) where a person lives
2. A family living together in one building, house, etc.
3. A place where something normally or naturally lives or is located
4. A familiar or usual setting: congenial environment
5. To a vital sensitive core (the truth struck home)
6. To a final, closed, or ultimate position. To or at an ultimate objective

Poem: Selection from "Healing the Mare" by Linda McCarriston

"As I soothe you I surprise wounds
of my own this long time unmothered.
As you stand, scathed and scabbed,
with your head up, I swab. As you
press, I lean into my own loving
touch, for which no wound
is too ugly."

Meal: Glass noodles and edamame, golden fried tofu; chocolate cream pie, lemon meringue pie

Prompt: Write about a moment you felt at home
By Mary

Right now. I feel at home right now, on this cozy couch, with these beautiful women who feel like comfort to me. They are now so familiar; they make me smile and I love them. As I write this, I look around, there is golden glowing light on either side of Surani and Jenny. We are all diligently writing from our hearts. I am having an ahh ha moment— "this is home". With these women, we are navigating this life- this wildlife and it feeds my soul.

I am finding more and more times that the experience of HOME is when I allow myself to be in my heart.

Which translate to coming from love. "Fear is the cheapest room in the house. I would like to see you living in better conditions" (Hafiz) So, letting go of the niggling worry, relaxing and allowing the playfulness—is home.

Last week, did a home visit to a patient I love. She and her family asked me to stay for dinner. I let go of my "professional aura" to be present, human and it was lovely. They were so sweet. Yummy food. It felt like home.

Saturday, with Melissa, Dion, Ara, Bruce and I. We became a unit. Moving in almost unspoken unison of love and support "You need this? Let's do that" Not needing to be anywhere else- happy, content, relaxed. No craving. Acceptance is home.

Back to present. The deep connectedness of this group. By writing from a prompt- I see that we are supporting each other to more fully be ourselves, owning our lives, bridging differences, and capturing the richness of what it means to be serving other humans in the ways we do.

Our hearts have been friends for a very long time. It helps to have a happy belly while doing the writing and connecting. This is home.

01/15/2019

Word: Impeachment

Defined in Merriam Webster:
1. To charge (a public official) with a crime done while in office
2. Formal: to cause doubts about the truthfulness of (a witness, testimony, etc.)
3. To cast doubt on; specially to challenge the credibility or validity of

Poem: Taken from "The White House" by Claude McKay (1889-1948)

"Oh, I must search for wisdom every hour,
deep in my wrathful bosom sore and raw,
and find in it the superhuman power
to hold me to the letter of your law!
Oh, I must keep my heart inviolate
against the potent poison of your hate."

Meal: Pumpkin stew with couscous, Caesar salad, peach/mint pie, mint chocolate chip ice cream

Recipe: Pumpkin Soup with Couscous

1 tablespoon extra-virgin olive oil

1 small onion, peeled & chopped finely

2 garlic cloves, finely chopped

½ teaspoon ground turmeric

½ teaspoon ground ginger

½ teaspoon ground cumin

¼ teaspoon ground cinnamon

¼ teaspoon ground cardamon

1/8 teaspoon cayenne pepper

2 cups vegetable stock

1 can pumpkin puree (15 oz) or 2 cups fresh, pureed

2 tablespoons pure maple syrup

Juice from half a lemon (2 tablespoons)

Cashew cream sauce (1 cup-soaked cashews blended with ½ cup non-dairy milk

1 teaspoon kosher salt & fresh black pepper

INSTRUCTIONS:

Heat olive oil in a large skillet and add in the chopped onion and garlic. Cook on low to medium heat for about 5 minutes being careful not to burn. Add all the spices and stir well. Heat for a couple of minutes on low.

Add in vegetable stock, pumpkin puree, maple syrup, and lemon juice. Stir well. Simmer on low-medium for 15 minutes.

Make the cashew cream sauce by blending 1 cup of cashews that have soaked in water for at least 1 hour. Add in ½ cup of milk into the blender and blend until smooth. Scoop out and add ¾ of this cashew sauce into the soup. Stir and reserve the rest for garnish on top of the bowl. Heat for another 5 minutes and then serve immediately over couscous. Sprinkle with Pepita seeds if desired.

Prompt: Write about your experience with hate…
By Surani

I can still remember the sensation of burning shame.
My whole body was on fire with anger.
Pure hatred.
The feeling of part of my *self*
not being me.
And not wanting it to be me.
Wishing so hard that any god would hear my appeal.
That. This. Had. Not. Happened.
But it had and I had to steel myself to bear it.
To not show anything in my face.
Because showing would mean losing.
And I was not going to lose this.
I remember not wanting to move for an hour or more. I didn't change my clothes or touch my hair.
I was still in shock this had happened.
I was not the same.
Not like everyone else.
I burned with hatred; I felt like I would explode.
I would have slain you with my eyes if possible.
I swore I would never forget this.

And I would never tolerate this for anyone. Ever.

Your callous, stupid gesture showed your hatred of me, my skin, my body.

I refused to ever wear the jacket again- the site of your spittle dripping slowly down my back could never be erased.

I scrubbed my hair so hard that night, trying to remove the memory of your hatred.

I hope you are rotting in a hell of your own making. No child, no person should ever feel like this.

The hatred.

The shame.

I impeach your stupidity.

06/11/2013

Word: Joy

Defined in Merriam Webster:
1. (a) the emotion evoked by well-being, success, or good fortune or by the prospect of possessing what one desires: DELIGHT
    (b) the expression or exhibition of such emotion: GAIETY
2. A state of happiness or felicity: BLISS
3. A source or cause of delight
4. To experience great pleasure or delight: REJOICE

Poem: (not archived)

Meal: Vegetarian enchilada, beet salad, green salad, guacamole; Chocolate brownies, banana ice cream, caramel ice cream, lemon cheesecake, chocolate éclair, fruit tart, napoleon

Prompt: A time when my heart sang......
By Penny

March 17, 1971, I had been in hard labor for 19 hours. I keep telling myself "I can do this. It must be alright. Every person on earth comes in this way and I am bringing this baby here. Yea, a few don't make it, but I can do it, I can do it, I can do it...." I am exhausted!

I am now in the delivery room. The doctor keeps telling me to push...I think to myself "I am pushing!!! What does he think I am doing?" He says these words again and again. In my head I am screaming "I am! I am!" The doctor then starts helping by pressing on my diaphragm until I feel like I cannot breathe. Then I hear "the head is through". And then the announcement "You have a baby boy".

I am elevated to another reality. There is this beautiful light that fills the room. I feel a sense of elation that is other worldly. I have no pain, no fatigue, only the joy of participating in a true miracle.

06/23/2020

Word: Loneliness

Defined in Merriam Webster:
1. Sad from being alone Producing a feeling of bleakness or desolation
2. Cut ff from others
3. Without frequent contact with other human beings

Poem: From *"Multitudinous Stars"* by Ping Hsin (Translated from Chinese by Kenneth Rexroth and Chung Ling

"…These fragmented verses
Are only drops of spray
On the sea of knowledge.
Yet they are bright shining
Multitudinous star, inlaid
On the skies of the heart.
Bright moon---
All grief, sorrow, loneliness completed—"

Meal: (Not shared because of Zoom) Roasted salmon, roasted asparagus with browned butter, lemon and pistachios

Prompt: Write about a time when loneliness departed.
By Surani

It is interesting how little loneliness one has in life at the beginning. You are literally never alone, always having a parent/caregiver at your beck and call.

It is interesting to experience loneliness for the first time.

The time your parent steps out of the house and you don't see them go.

The feeling of rising panic as you cannot find them in the empty rooms; the sense you are lost,

directionless.

This must be true loneliness.

Loss, fear, and no hope.

Then the flood of relief when your parent reappears, almost magically. The relief is like being caught in a wave- it crushes you until you almost can't breathe.

You feel joy,

and the future.

It is only later that you feel anger at the abandonment.

How could this have happened?

When did this happen?

Will this happen again?

And then, just as quickly, we forget all those feelings, emotions.

Or maybe

They are built into our cells, like honey stored in honeycomb.

Being alone can be relished.

Loneliness is sorrow- the opposite of joy when loneliness is lifted.

03/27/2018

Word: Mystery

Defined in Merriam Webster:
1. Profound, inexplicable, or secretive quality or character
2. (a) something not understood or beyond understanding
   (b) a piece of fiction dealing usually with the solution of a mysterious crime
   (c) the secret or specialized practices or ritual peculiar to an occupation or a body of people
   (d) obsolete: a private secret
3. (a) a religious truth that one can know only by revelation and cannot fully understand
   (b) 1- any of the 20 events serving as a subject for meditation during the saying of the rosary
   2- the Christian sacrament
   (c) 1- a secret religious rite believed to impart enduring bliss to the initiate
   2- a cult devoted to such rites

Poem: Selection for "Nani "by Alberto Rios, printed in 1982 in "Whispering to Fool the Wind"
"...*I see a wrinkle speak*
of a man whose body serves
the ants like she serves me, then more words
from more wrinkles about children, words
about this and that, flowing more
easily from these other mouths. Each serves
as a tremendous string around her,

holding her together."…

Meal: Pasta with two types of noodles, red sauce, Bean salad; Meyer Lemon cake with diorama of the start of Life, Ice cream

Prompt: Write about a time when you didn't understand.
By Chris

I can't help but write in the vein of the mood of the poem we just read-- a dimly lit kitchen, or room, or hut, with an elder person with wrinkles, who spoke words I did not understand. We were in a village in the Highlands of Guatemala, and we said ok to the opportunity to visit the village shaman or curandero. We had to pay 40 quetzales, and purchase candles, and liquor and sodas and something else like soap on the way to his home. Our guide had to waken the old man who was in bed already, in his dark home—one room really, which was dominated by a wall of statues of saints, candles, flowers and colors—the whole wall was an altar. The house was lit only by candles.

The curandero only spoke his indigenous dialect, and he looked very, very old. We felt funny getting him out of bed for our touristic adventure. He seemed quite happy, though. He asked us what we wanted or needed, and we said we need help with our relationship. He started the ritual and it went on and on and on, with many prayers and offerings and spitting of alcohol, breaking of eggs, offerings to this saint and then that one, all catholic in this ancient ritual show, all to help our relationship. It was dark, the words and songs were unknown to me; it was a picture out of time, we were definitely getting our 40 quetzals worth, and I hoped the shaman was as well! I looked around the room/house—there was a raised pallet for his bed, and many sacks of corn pouring out of burlap bags. Lots of clutter; piles of clothes and blankets, but little else that I could really see.

The ritual ended after a very long time. We were well prayed for. We left the old man with the guide not knowing what really had happened or what he had said to those saints and gods.

The next day, on the streets in the marketplace, we saw the old curandero walking with his cane. We went up to him and he recognized us with a big smile. He said lots of words to us again, but what I understood was the one Spanish word: "amable, amable"—I got it, he was saying "be kind to each other, be kind".

08/07/2019

Word: Nurse

Merriam Webster defines:
1. A person who cares for the sick or infirmed.
2. Specifically: a licensed health-care professional who practices independently or is supervised by a physician, surgeon, or dentist and who is skilled in promoting and maintaining health
3. One that looks after, fosters, or advises
4. To nourish at the breast: SUCKLE
5. To care for and wait on (someone, such as a sick person)
6. To attempt to cure by care and treatment
   (a) to manage with care or economy
   (b) to promote the development or progress of (c) to take charge of and watch over

Poem: Selections from Florence Nightengale (born May 12, 1820 & died August 13, 1910) "notes on Nursing" ("Effect of Body on Mind")

Volumes are now written and spoken upon the effect of the mind upon the body. Much of it is true. But I wish a little more was thought of the effect of the body on the mind. You who believe yourselves overwhelmed with anxieties, but are able every day to walk up Regent-street, or out in the country, to take your meals with others in other rooms, &c., &c., you little know how much your anxieties are thereby lightened; you little know how intensified they become to those who can have no changes;

* how the very walls of their sick rooms seem hung with their cares; how the ghosts of their troubles haunt their beds; how impossible it is for them to escape from a pursuing thought without some help from variety.

A patient can just as much move his leg when it is fractured as change his thoughts to when no external help from variety is given him. This is indeed, one of the main sufferings of sickness; just

* It is a matter of painful wonder to the sick themselves how much painful ideas predominate over pleasurable ones in their impressions; they reason with themselves; they think themselves ungrateful; it is all of no use. The fact is that these painful impressions are far better dismissed by a real laugh, if you can excite one by book or conversation, than by any direct reasoning; or if the patient is too weak to laugh, some impression from nature is what he wants. I have mentioned the cruelty of letting him stare at a dead wall. In many diseases, especially in convalescence from fever, that wall will appear to make all sorts of faces at him; now flowers never do this. Form, colour, will free your patient from his painful ideas better than say argument.as the fixed posture is one of the main sufferings of the broken limb.

It is an ever-recurring wonder to see educated people, who call themselves nurses, acting thus. They vary their own objects, their own employments many times a day; and while nursing(!) some bed-ridden sufferer, they let him lie there staring at a dead wall, without any change of object to enable him to vary his thoughts; and it never even occurs to them, at least to move his bed so that he can look out of window. No, the bed is to always left in the darkest, dullest, remotest part of the room.

I think it is a very common error among the well to think that "with a little more self-control" the sick might, if they choose "dismiss painful thoughts" which "aggravate their disease, &c.

Believe me, almost any sick person, who behaves decently well, exercises more self-control every moment of his day than you will ever know till you are sick yourself. Almost every step that crosses his room is painful to him; almost every thought that crosses his brain is painful to him; and if he can speak without be savage, and look without being unpleasant, he is exercising self-control.

Suppose you have been up all night, and instead of being allowed to have your cup of tea, you were to be told that you ought to "exercise self-control," what should you say? Now, the nerves of the sick are always in the state that yours are in after you have been up all night.

Meal: Indian/ Nepalese food. Paneer with garbanzo beans, rice, watermelon salad, green salad, blueberry cake.

PANEER with Garbanzo Beans
RECIPE:
1 ¼ cups dried chickpeas (3 ¾ cups cooked)
4 tablespoons ghee or oil
1 cup paneer cheese, cut into bite size cubes

4 cloves garlic, crushed or minced

1-inch fresh ginger, grated or minced

1 teaspoon cumin seeds

1 bay leaf, crumbled

2-3 fresh chilies, finely chopped

2 teaspoons ground coriander

1 ½ teaspoons ground cumin

½ teaspoon turmeric

½ teaspoon cayenne

1 teaspoon sea salt

Fresh cracked black pepper to taste

1 large tomato, diced

Juice from 1 lemon (3 tablespoons)

½ teaspoon garam masala

INSTRUCTIONS:

Rinse the chickpeas and soak for 8 hours or overnight in several inches of water. Drain and rinse, then transfer to a large saucepan and cover with 4 cups of fresh water. Bring to a boil, reduce heat to low, cover, and simmer for 1 to 2 hours or until the chickpeas are buttery soft. Drain and reserve 1 cup of the cooking liquid.

Meanwhile, heat 2 tablespoons of the ghee or oil in a non-stick pan over medium heat. When hot, add the paneer cubes and gently fry, turning often, until the cubes are nicely browned on all sides. Remove with a slotted spoon and set aside.

Heat the remaining ghee or oil over medium heat in a large saucepan. When hot, add the onion, garlic and ginger and sauté until the onions are browned. Add the cumin seeds and bay leaf, let sizzle for a few seconds, then add the chilies, ground coriander, ground cumin, turmeric, cayenne, salt, and pepper, and stir for another minute. Stir in the tomato and cook for 2 to 3 minutes.

Now add ½ cup of the reserved chickpea cooking liquid and stir in the cooked chickpeas and fried paneer cubes. Cook gently for another 5-8 minutes, adding more liquid to desired consistency. When the dish is nearly done, stir in the lemon juice and garam masala. Serve hot.

Makes 4 to 6 servings.

Prompt: "Write about your nurse self"
By Mary

What is my nurse self? It is me. I have grown into this. Nursing has been my greatest university. Yes, it is an honor and a privilege to closely behold the wings and shallows of humanity. And, it has also brought me to my knees, many times. The battle between "do I show up in full authenticity to witness, to be with? Or do I hide behind a cloak of clinic-ability?"

At times, the hiding offers some refuge, but it never lands right in my soul. So, I have shown up, over and over, at times in heart wrenching places, such as, providing home infusion care for many years, mostly tending to beautiful young men dying of AIDS.

My heart was pulled and stretched and became so much stronger, sturdier, and sore.

What is a nurse self? Medicine and healing combine many things. A collaboration of doctoring and nursing. Look up "to nurse a drink". It states you hold it carefully as if it was a child, you stay with it. "To doctor a drink" is to change it, to alter it with a substance or something else". This isn't to diminish physicians as I have gotten to work with and be supported by many absolutely exemplary doctors. With nursing, I learned to be with, to stay with, to hold, to bear loving witness.

I found one of the most important things for someone who is dying is that they know they aren't alone, that someone is staying and holding. A story- I was co-managing a home hospice patient with a morphine pump. Arrived at his home to check on it and him. He was alone in the front room hospital bed, agitated, Cheyne-Stokes breathing, very uncomfortable and actively dying. The family, who loved him dearly, were too afraid to be with him. They were just behind the kitchen door- 4 of them. I got it they didn't know how to be with him, he couldn't die alone. I set up between his bed and the kitchen door. I used moist cloths on his forehead. I asked the family "what do you want him to hear?" They told me things to say to him, I was the relay. They eventually started talking directly to him thru the door, he calmed. He became more peaceful, not agitated. His family cried. They told stories. One daughter had a belated apology. There was some singing. I was telling him it was ok to go, while tears were streaming. After about an hour, his breathing slowed, calm, and slow, then stopped. The room, which already felt so filled with grace, became lighter. The family came out around him to hug and hold him. To bathe him. To be with him.

Roshi Joan Halifax states that to be present in the world, one needs a soft front and a strong back. This is so true with nursing. Being there with an open, compassionate heart is much of the healing journey. And it takes courage to show up, building strong back muscles have helped me. But also, I have found that the most profound action is to surrender, become a vessel, allow life/ spirit/ my father would call "the Holy Ghost", to move through me as that is where the deepest wisdom comes from. So my nursing self are the best parts of me. At this point, I have been a nurse for 40 of my 65 years. As I said in my intro, I have worked in so many settings. I've helped babies be born and helped people die, and all kinds of things in between! I travelled, worked in clinics in India, Nepal, Mexico. I have seen that behind the eyes of each person is a deep, individual, complex story. AND that we are also so much the same. We are sparks from a common source. The glory of this understanding and the luck of learning a skill that puts me in the midst of this great mystery makes me feel profoundly fortunate to have a "nurse self".

Prompt: Write about your nurse self.

By Maria

I have two writings on this. One I wrote at our meeting and the other, I wrote a couple of months later as I processed a challenging situation at work.

My Nurse Self

Flowing of thoughts, pain, experiences
In the process of healing
Always healing, moving towards the golden sun
Surrounded by love, supported in nature
I am moving
I am healing
I share with others this gift to see,
To almost taste their world
We merge and sometimes we come out the other side imprinted
Changed for the better
As if our cells were somehow rearranged and
We are different
The stories are still there
History has not changed
But what we have
There is less pain, and we are opened
A small crack allows love to flow inside us
You and me
It holds us and reminds us that
We are good
We are alive

A life worth living
This love heals us
We heal each other
Tired yet stronger

With this we move forward till we see someone else in pain, again
And we share with them this secret, which isn't really a secret because

It exists to be given

This is my nurse self. It isn't just myself but I am part of so much
more

Pain and love and pain and love and joy and love and wonder and
love and

YOU

NURSE 10/20/2019

I received a Sudden Infant Death Syndrome (SIDS) referral last week. These referrals require follow up from the SIDS Coordinator at Public Health. The last sentence on the referral stated that the case was "suspicious" and "under investigation". There was even a case number. Well, hmmmmm, I'm not the "real SIDS Coordinator" and was filling in for my supervisor who was on leave.

Fun fact, in Sonoma county we had not had a SIDS death since 2017. In August, when our Coordinator went on leave, I received two referrals and another one last week!!!

Me and dying babies.... What does that mean, I wonder? I thought I had my fill of dying babies with my two second trimester miscarriages.

"This is different" some deep aspect of my essence told me.

According the State SIDS Protocol, the SIDS Coordinator reaches out to the family within 72 hours of the infant's death. The Public Health Nurse, gathers information, completes the State SIDS form, offers resources, support and a home visit. Simple enough, intense but simple.

The first two referrals were intense because I had never done this before and I know the pain of losing a baby. It's so unfair! But somehow, I got through it with the help of kind Coroner's Office Sergeant (Adrian) and the wisdom of our ex-MCAH Director Norma. Yes, I needed two people to help me get through this.

It goes deep.

This recent referral, however, is more complicated. It is "under investigation", "suspicious" and I do not want to interfere with that. Many thoughts and situations are floating in my brain, taking turns elevating my cortisol level.

Is it safe for me to go on a home visit? Is it "suspicious" because someone hurt the baby? The father was caring for the baby when he became unresponsive. Did he hurt his son? If I go to their home will he hurt me?

What if I just meet with the mom?

Back to the word "nurse". A nurse is compassionate, non-threatening, we are good listeners, patient and supportive. I have seen people at their most vulnerable moments: scared, pre/post-surgery, after a traumatic event. I have listened as they shared their dying wish and held their hand as they slip into another world. I have been there after they gave birth and watched them shift into mama bear mode. I have cared for patients after heart surgery, they have told me of their experience on the "other side". I taught patients to walk again after a hip and knee replacements. Nurses are there for those moments. We are present. We are open. We are connected.

My dilemma with the SIDS case is that if I speak to the mom, will she trust me and share personal information about their family which may implicate someone in the case? Do I then need to testify because I was able to listen to the mom and accept her story? Because she was comfortable with me and able to share her pain and fear?

All these thoughts from one piece of paper. Each word weighted by strong emotions. These words trigger scenarios in my head. These scenarios which spin my mind into dizziness........

I need to help her.

She's in pain and needs me.

It's my obligation to respond.

72 hours

What time is it?

How do I proceed?

My babies died too.

So much pain.

My little girls,

so little.

Where do I go from here?

Will I be able to talk to her without crying?

Norma ----- my hero Norma helps me ground. She supports my ideas on how to proceed. She's so calm. HOW DOES SHE DO THAT?!?!?!

Contact the state SIDS Coordinator.

Yes, send the grief support information to the family by mail.

Have the coroner's office contact us when the case is closed and then reach out to the family directly.

Then they can talk with me and share what they need.

The pain.

The knowledge that they are not alone.

The knowledge that their sweet son is now an angel watching over them.

04/16/2019

Word: Pleasure

Merriam Webster defines as:
1. DESIRE, INCLINATION
2. A state of gratification
3. A source of delight or joy

Poem: Selection from *"This Is Just to Say"* William Carolos Williams
"I have eaten
the plums
that were in
the icebox…"

Meal: Mushroom Risotto, Veggie Kabobs with Cheese sauce, Salad, Chocolate Fondue

Recipe: Mushroom Risotto:

6 cups of vegetable broth, divided

3 tablespoons olive oil, divided

1-pound portobello mushrooms, thinly sliced

1-pound white mushrooms, thinly sliced

2 shallots, diced

1 ½ cups Arborio rice

½ cup dry white wine

Sea salt to taste. Fresh ground black pepper to taste

4 tablespoons finely chopped chives

4 tablespoons butter

1/3 cup freshly grated Parmesan cheese

INSTRUCTIONS:

In a saucepan, warm the broth over low heat.

Warm 2 tablespoons olive oil in a large saucepan over medium-high heat. Stir in the mushrooms, and cook until soft, about 3 minutes. Remove mushrooms and their liquid and set aside.

Add 1 tablespoon olive oil to skillet and stir in the shallots. Cook 1 minutes. Add rice, stirring to coat with oil, about 2 minutes. When the rice has taken on a pale, golden color, pour in wine, stirring constantly until the wine is fully absorbed. Add ½ cup broth to the rice and stir until the broth is absorbed. Continue adding broth ½ cup at a time, stirring continuously until the liquid is absorbed and rice is al dente, about 15-20 minutes.

Remove from heat and stir in mushrooms with their liquid, butter, chives, and parmesan. Season with salt and pepper to taste.

Prompt: Write about a moment when you just had to have it…
By Surani

I made a vow to a friend. We were in this together.

The days stretched in front of me like *years*. How was I going to do this?

I could do this!

Control the desire.

The craving.

I was committed to you and our vow.

The first day was easy. Feeling self-righteous with myself. No big deal.

The first week was terrible. I found myself negotiating away the guilt.

What did it matter? Nothing rested on this agreement- really...

The yearning.

The headaches.

Did I actually feel better?

Was I just kidding myself?

By thirty days I was convinced it wouldn't matter.

I was in a slow-motion slide towards guilt.

Of broken promises.

Because I. Could. Not. Control the desire.

And then one day, I decide- "f%@* it- I'm going for it!

Plus I don't want to waste it.

I get out the perfect container.

I smell the faint promise to come.

I can almost feel it now.

The heat rises fast and wafts over me.

Then it is a satisfying experience of a favorite cup.

Just the right size.

And then the first sip... from the spoon because it is hot.

The divine pleasure of hot chocolate- making the day a joy.

Prompt: Write a moment when you just had to have it...
By Shari

I hate to tell you how many animals I have brought home without ever asking anyone else in the house, including my patient husband how they felt about it, or asked their opinion about whether they though that it was a good idea. The donkeys were the largest and the silliest. I was not looking for them, but I heard that there was a pair of elderly donkeys needed a new home because their owners were moving out of state. I just wanted to look at them though my friend, Trina, knew what I was up to. It was probably their ears that got to me; their big soft, fuzzy ears. they were a bit dusty, but Cassie came right over and I swear he put his head in my lap and I touched his soft nose. Before I remember, I was making arrangements to have them brought to my home. we had a fenced pasture, but I would need a shelter for them. They needed a bath I thought, to get rid of some of the dust. (I didn't realize that they would always be dusty because they rolled in the dust constantly). Cassie still puts his head against my chest and gazes at me with his big brown eyes and Jimmy who kicks you when you try to trim his hooves but he kicks up his heels with joy and races around the pasture for the fun of it. They make me smile.

11/13/2018

Word: Precious

Defined in Merriam Webster:
1. Rare and worth a lot of money
2. Very valuable or important: too valuable or important to be wasted or used carelessly
3. Greatly loved, valued, or important

Poem: Selection from "Everything is Plundered..." by Anna Akhmatova (1889-1966)
translated by Stanley Kunitz with Max Hayward
"...at night the deep transparent skies
glitter with new galaxies.
And the miraculous comes so close
to the ruined, dirty houses---
something not known to anyone at all,
but wild in our breast for centuries."

Meal: Udon soup- tofu, veggies, hard-boiled egg; Spinach salad; Cupcakes, Moochie

Prompt: What is wild in your heart....
By Shari

From all time I can remember, I have yearned for the wilderness, for nature, for animals, the smell of dirt and grass, rivers, streams, lakes, and mountains. Swimming underwater in clear rivers or lakes - that is my joy (best naked).

My parents tried to tame me no doubt. They weren't excessively proper - just middle-class suburban - there were things you say and don't say, be clean, dress nicely.

I admit I enjoyed going to San Francisco every Fall to shop with my mom and grandmother to get 3 new outfits for school- only dresses and skirts in those days. I loved picking out new clothes and going to lunch in San Francisco. I tried, I really tried to look good when we went to the city, it was a time when you dressed up to go, I had on my best shoes, white gloves, a little purse, but I quickly ended up losing my purse while riding get some escalator at Macy's or Joseph Magnums. White socks dirty, somehow got dirty, and I looked like I just swept out a chimney. I liked to touch everything and sit on the floor, dresses got ripped - school ruined my clothes even faster- dirt fields and monkey bars, kick ball, pretending to be a horse took up much of my life. Actually, pretty much all I thought about was horses and life in the country.

I remember the slopes of Mt Tam, fields to play in and just feeling such excitement, getting down low in the green grass, bug level, to watch the smallness of things and the smell of dirt. When we went to Lake Tahoe for a week's vacation in the summer and I got to go horseback riding that was pure joy, the smell of pine needles and horse manure in the sun. That was where I was at home. Where does that come from? I seemed to be born that way and can't remember any other way of being or ever wanting to live in a city. Now when I wake up in the morning to the trees and bird song, so many years later, I smile.

4/10/2018

Word: Presence

Defined in Merriam Webster:
1. The fact or condition of being present
   (a) the part of space within one's immediate vicinity
   (b) the neighborhood of one of superior especially royal rank
2. one that is present
3. something (such as a spirit) felt or believed to be present
4. (a) the bearing, carriage, or air of a person
   (b) a noteworthy quality of poise and effectiveness

Poem: Selection from "Tornados" by Thylias Moss
"...*Ions played*
instead of notes. The movement
is not wrath, not hormone swarm because
I saw my first forming above the church a surrogate
steeple. The morning of my first baptism and
salvation already tangible, funnel for the spirit
coming into me without losing a drop, my black
guardian angel come to rescue me before all the words
get out, I looked over Jordan and what did I see coming for
to carry me home."

Meal: Salmon puff pastry pockets, green salad; Raspberry tart
Recipe: Salmon Puff Pastry Pockets
2 tablespoons olive oil
2 medium shallots, finely chopped
9 ounces cremini mushrooms, sliced into ¼ inch thick slices

6 ounces baby spinach leaves

Kosher salt and freshly ground black pepper

All purpose flour, for rolling out the pastry

2 sheets frozen puff pastry, thawed

1 large egg, beaten

2-pound salmon fillet, skinless

Dill Sauce:

2/3 cup clam juice

¾ cup Mexican crema

½ cup heavy cream

2 teaspoons all-purpose flour

3 tablespoons minced fresh dill

Kosher salt and freshly ground black pepper to taste

INSTRUCTIONS:

For the salmon: Preheat oven to 425 degrees F. Line a baking sheet with foil and spray with a nonstick cooking spray.

Heat the oil in a heavy sauté pan over medium-high heat. Add the shallots and cook until translucent and fragrant, about 2 minutes. Add the mushrooms and cook until the liquid evaporates, about 3 minutes. Add the spinach and wilt for 4 minutes. Season the mixture with salt and pepper. Let cool.

Dust a flat working surface with flour. Using a rolling pin, roll out the sheets of puff pastry into 1/4 -inch thickness (each 12 by 12 inches). Put the pastry sheets side by side so they overlap slightly, by about ½ inch. Brush the overlapping strip with the beaten egg, stick both sheets together at the strip and seal with a fork. Transfer to the prepared baking sheet.

Spoon the cooled mushroom-spinach mixture over one side of the puff pastry rectangle. To make an even rectangle out of the salmon fillet, you can cut the top portion off the belly and add it to the tail portion. Place the salmon fillet over the mushroom-spinach mixture. Season the salmon heavily with salt and pepper. Fold the other side of the rectangle over the filling and seal by brushing the edge with egg and crimp the edge using a fork (like the edge of pie crust). Fold the remaining 2 open edges of pastry under the salmon fillet. Brush everything with the remaining beaten egg.

Bake until the puff pastry is crisp and golden in color, approximately 25 minutes. Let stand for about 8 minutes before slicing.

Slice the salmon into 1 ½-inch slices. Serve immediately with the dill sauce.

Dill Sauce Instructions:
Put the clam juice in a heavy saucepot and bring to a boil. Lower to a simmer and reduce to ½ cup. Add the Mexican crema and heavy cram and reduce liquid to 1 cup. Add the flour and whisk while boiling until thickened. Add the dill and season with salt and pepper.

Prompt: A time when you experienced a presence…
By Shari

"So many questions" I want help but go with the presence of someone who visited on their way to a different place because it is the first thing that comes. Although I know I have spoken of this before, the passing of the dead and the gift that was given twice in my life. I want more true, but I am happy to have these, maybe it's from a parallel universe that someone slips through briefly. I don't know and never will but it's still a gift that I want to pass on to my pass on to my children, the comfort of that, but they seem to want none of it. they kind of roll their eyes when I speak of such things. Proof is what they want and I can't give it. I can't give anyone faith. How do I explain a feeling, a sparkle, a little rip in the fabric that the light comes through?

The time my father came to me after he died, found his way to me, I had a feeling of sadness and someone/ something touching my hair, pulling it back into a ponytail like he used to do. Later I found out he had died about that same time. what did I feel? I can't tell you but it still soothes me and gives me hope of us, of our souls' essence beyond our bodies. and the one other time when Alex died (my brother I law) I felt the light change or something changed and I felt the deepest peace I have ever known for a few seconds/ minutes and found out Alex had died at just that time. I felt that he was giving me a gift of hope, of God. MAYBE but thank you. We struggled with our relationship in life but he gave me that anyway.

Oh and then there was that weird trail of light and movement that the dogs followed on the trail through the forest leading to our house. Was that scent made visible? A streak they sensed and followed and I got a glimpse of and stared at in amazement, a ghost dog?

Prompt: A time when I experienced a presence...
By Penny

This was 1965. I was 15 years old in Washington DC with my 18-year-old male cousin. My Aunt and Uncle had invited me to join them on this vacation across the country in a Volkswagen Bug to attend my other older cousin's wedding, their son, in NYC. The trip was to be fun, purposeful, and educational. We would stop and see many historic sites and visit some relatives of my Uncle's in Canada and cousin's I had never met on my mother and Aunt's side in North Dakota.

On this day in Washington, DC we were on our way to attend a Senate meeting. My cousin and I were going our own way to get there, and we stepped into an elevator going up to the Senate floor. The day was already charged with such energy, such wonder and grandeur of being in the Nation's Capital. The awe of history surrounding us, surrounding me.

The elevator door opens, and Robert Kennedy and Ted Kennedy enter our elevator. I can't breathe. I start crying, tears streaming down my cheeks. I want to touch them and tell them how sad I am the John was killed; how wrong it was. The tears keep streaming and burning face. Robert turns around and asks; "Are you alright? Is this your first time here?" My cousin is so embarrassed to be with me now, I could tell.

I have a program in my hands for the day's Senate Agenda. All I could do was ask, "Would you sign my program?" I think I am going to faint. These two iconic men are in my space, and I am sharing their "presence".

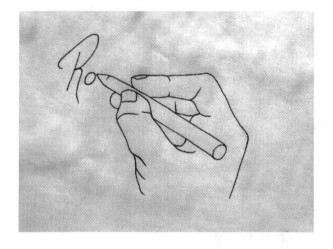

8-14-2018

Word: Resilience

Defined in Merriam Webster:
1. The capability of a strained body to recover its size and shape after deformation caused especially by compressive stress
2. An ability to recover from or adjust easily to misfortune or change

Poem: Selection from "Root Cellar" by Theodore Roethke (1908-1963)
"…And what a congress of stinks!—
Roots ripe as old bait,
Leaf-mold, manure, lime, piled against slippery planks.
Nothing would give up life:
Even the dirt kept breathing a small breath."

Meal: Gado gado, satay sauce, Quinoa salad, Green salad, Buttermilk Brown Butter cake, Strawberries

GADO GADO RECIPE:

Rice:

2 cups short grain brown rice, rinsed

4 cups water

Vegetables:

2 large, sweet potatoes, rinsed and chopped into ¼-inch thick slices

2 tablespoons avocado oil

1-pound green beans, stems removed

1 medium red bell pepper, thinly sliced

1 ½ cups bean sprouts

Peanut Sauce:

½ cup natural salted peanut butter

2 tablespoons tamari

3-4 tablespoons fresh lime juice

3-4 tablespoons maple syrup

5-6 teaspoons chili garlic sauce

4-6 tablespoons hot water

For Serving:

Garnish with fresh chopped cilantro

1/3 cup roasted salted peanuts

Sliced hard-boiled egg

INSTRUCTIONS:

In a large saucepan, bring water and brown rice to a boil, then add a pinch of salt and swirl to combine, cover and reduce heat to simmer. Cook for 30-40 minutes until water is absorbed and rice is tender and fully cooked. Drain off any excess liquid at the end if there is any. Set rice aside and cover to keep warm.

In the meantime, preheat oven to 400 degrees F and line a baking sheet with parchment paper. Add sliced sweet potato and drizzle with avocado oi. Bake for 20-25 minutes. When ready, rounds should be tender and slightly golden brown. Set aside.

While potato rounds and rice are cooking, steam green beans in a steamer basket or in the microwave for 3-4 minutes.

Prepare the peanut sauce by adding all ingredients except water to a small mixing bowl and whisk. Add hot water 1 tablespoon at a time until desired consistency is reached. Sauce should be pourable.

Taste and adjust seasonings as needed, adding more chili garlic sauce for heat, maple syrup for sweetness or lime juice for acidity.

To assemble, divide brown rice between dishes and top with roasted sweet potato, steamed green beans, sliced red pepper, bean sprouts, cilantro, and a hard-boiled egg. Serve with spicy peanut sauce and salted roasted peanuts. For extra heat, sriracha or extra chili garlic sauce may be added.

Best when served fresh. Store any leftovers separate from dressing in the refrigerator up to 2 days.

Writing Prompt: A time when you made it through the darkness
By Surani

Driving at night has that feeling- like you are alone in the world, everything around you is asleep.
No one is aware of you
Or cares.
Solitary.
Time to think,
lots of time to think and the overhead light will occasionally lighten up the interior
Bright as day.
It's not unlike the experience of moving through something
A horrible event or awful experience.

The feeling of being alone in the world, nothing around you is aware (of you) or cares.

And every once in awhile- a bright flash or even a glimmer of something good

Or better.

A memory of how good

Is.

And you want to reach out- drag yourself closer to the sense of something better, warm

Welcoming.

Calamity happens to all of us and we all experience it differently,

But the sense of withdrawing and then returning is somehow the condition of our mind

Refusing to give up.

Resilience.

Word: Risk

Defined in Merriam Webster:

1. Possibility of loss or injury: PERIL
2. Someone or something that creates or suggests a hazard
   (a) the chance of loss or the perils to the subject matter of an insurance contract
   (b) a person or thing that is a specified hazard to an insurer
   (c) an insurance hazard from a specified cause or source
3. the chance that an investment will lose value (such as a stock or commodity

(Poem, meal, date, and prompt were not saved for this writing.)
By Jenny

I sat with her, an angry, terrified daughter, who lived with her mama for 30 years. Mom, 101 years old was stunned, shut down by a stroke in May. The daughter hates and distrusts all aspects of medicine—wants her mom to die when ready but not from cellulitis. We agonized, 911? A trial of antibiotics here in the home? The hospital was her idea of hell for her mother. We both knew they would jump all over her. "Litigiousness'" oozed from every pore of the daughter.

It was one of those times when I didn't know the answer. This woman, tachypneic, non-responsive, moaning, red hot leg. It was like waiting with someone in labor, do you intervene? Do you… what?! Me, I didn't know the answer. We sat. We drank water, we looked at the patient, her mother, again. There was a vast space and I couldn't see the bridge. I knew I was holding the power, that next step. We wavered, back and forth…labor.

And then, everything melted away. I could hold the waiting and the answer came. Rocephin IM, a trial. Yes, I could see again, across the divide. The space closed.

I called Martha who met me at the Walgreens and she gave me a little brown bag with the Rocephin, lidocaine, 2 syringes and 3 needles. God you have to love nurses.

I went back to the moaning house, the sorrowing daughter and gave that woman a one-gram dose of Rocephin in her bottom. Then, we waited, and waited some more. 4 hours I was there. The breathing slowed, she cooled. We made it. I made it across my own divide.

05/12/2015

Word: Sisterhood

Defined in Merriam Webster:

1. A community or society of sisters
2. The solidarity of women based on shared conditions, experiences, or concerns
   (a) the state of being a sister
   (b) the sisterly relationship

Poem: Selection from "The Depths" by Denise Levertov in *The Jacob's Ladder,* New Directions, New York: 1958
"...After mist has wrapped us again
in fine wool, may the taste of salt
recall to us the great depths about us."

Meal: Vegan Enchiladas, salsa, salad, tortilla chips; chocolate-orange cake, chocolate bark

VEGAN ENCHILADAS RECIPE:
1 pound firm tofu drained, patted dry and cut into chunks
½ teaspoon kosher salt
½ teaspoon ground turmeric
¼ teaspoon ground cayenne pepper
2 tablespoons extra-virgin olive oil
2 medium jalapeno peppers, seeds and membranes removed, finely chopped
1 medium red bell pepper cored, seeded, and diced
1 small yellow onion finely diced

1 can black beans (15 ounces) rinsed and drained

1 packet frozen spinach (10 ounces) thawed and pressed dry

20 ounces red enchilada sauce (2 ½ cups)

18 small corn tortillas

For serving top with avocado slices, lime wedges and sliced radishes

INSTRUCTIONS:

Preheat oven to 350 degrees Fahrenheit

Lightly coat a large casserole dish with nonstick spray or olive oil and set aside.

Prepare the enchilada filling: Place the tofu in a food processor and puree for several minutes until smooth, stopping to scrape down the bowl as needed. Sprinkle in the salt, turmeric, black pepper, and cayenne. Pulse a few more times to mix well.

Heat the 2 tablespoons oil in a deep skillet over medium heat. Once hot and shimmering, add the jalapeno, bell pepper and onion. Cook, stirring occasionally, until vegetables soften and begin to brown, about 5 minutes. Stir in the tofu and cook until the tofu is heated through and dries somewhat (it should look like scrambled eggs), about 5 minutes. Stir in the beans and thawed, pressed spinach. Stir, breaking up the spinach as you go. Season with additional salt and pepper to taste.

Spoon a thin layer of the enchilada sauce into the bottom of the prepared baking dish. Wrap the tortillas in damp paper or cloth towel and microwave for 30 seconds to make them more pliable.

Scoop a ¼ cup portion of filling into each tortilla, roll tightly, and place seam-side down in the prepared baking dish. Repeat with remaining tortillas. Spoon the remaining enchilada sauce over the top of the enchiladas. Lightly coat any exposed tortillas with a little olive oil so they crisp nicely in the oven.

Bake for15 minutes, or until the sauce is hot and bubbly and tortillas are golden. Serve with topping.

Prompt: Write about a time when someone stood up for you…
By Jenny

I remember a really hard night in the ICN, as we called the NICU back then. The 24-weeker I had nurtured through so many storms, my first time as primary—my baby, so to speak. That night I pulled a double to try and pull him through and he didn't make it. I remember, I remember that tough faced, no shit nurse with the long brown ponytail who watched me—me, a ridiculous person for that mechanical, high wired world. What <u>was</u> I thinking, Miss "Feel everything, run screaming from anything electrical or with buttons and bells…."

I only knew I loved babies, god, I <u>was</u> a baby. But I was fierce and I tried and they watched me carefully, my new grad self. I was part of that coffee swilling, night shift team. As I stood there gripping the bars of the crib- the rest of the unit continuing the steady work of keeping the rest alive, she looked at me, slapped a 10 mg tablet of valium in my hand and said, "Go home. "In that moment, I understood that she had stood behind me and had watched every move I made, knew everything, stood and in 2 words, said, in essence, "You did good. I'm sorry. Here, you need this."

She was right, I did. I took it and slept and never forgot how in that terrible moment, I wasn't alone. Even though I was. She stood up for me and so did I.

4/9/2013

Word: Struggle

Defined in Merriam Webster:
1. To make strenuous or violent efforts in the face of difficulties or opposition
2. To proceed with difficulty or with great effort
3. A violent effort or exertion: an act of strongly motivated striving

Poem: (not archived)

Meal: Gado gado, peanut sauce, mango, cilantro, nuts, bean sprouts, cabbage; chocolate, chocolate cake

Prompt: A time when struggle took me nowhere, then somewhere.... By Penny

This is hard to pin down. I can think of many struggles that at the time seemed all consuming and of major importance, but in time each struggle morphed into a resolve, or resolution, or a transition to something that was a new or different level of awareness.

Like when my youngest son told me that he was moving to LA to live with his uncle because he was going to make it in the music business, he was 17. He had managed to fulfill all his requirements for graduation by the December before actual graduation with his class. He was ready to leave now. My total lack of reasonableness was equal to his determination to live this dream on his terms.

I struggled with him for several years over his decision. I was so scared for him and I lost my total faith and belief that he would be able to withstand the temptations of the lifestyle and environment he was putting himself in. Somehow, we both withstood this decision and come out with something different and rich. He lived his dream, avoided the pitfalls of drugs and alcohol. Somehow, I lived through these years and marvel at the man he has become.

10/20/2015

Word: Tunnel

Defined in Merriam Webster:

1. A hollow conduit or recess TUBE, WELL
   (a) a covered passageway
   (b) a subterranean gallery (as in a mine)
   (c) a burrow 2
2. to make or use a tunnel
3. physics: to pass through a potential barrier

Poem: (Poem not archived)

Meal: Lasagna rolls, Roasted vegetables, green salad; Cookies, strawberries, Chocolate

Prompt: Write about a time you went down a tunnel of freedom
By Chris

So, years later when my mother placed the food in the oven with the saran wrap on it, and years after that she said to me on my wedding day in the kitchen "Hi, I know I've met you but can't remember your name", and still years later they call me from the Sunrise Senior living and tell me she now needs to move to the Third Floor memory unit because she was found smearing cat feces on the walls...

The tunnel got narrower and narrower for her as her life marched on like a funnel so wide at the mouth, then smaller and smaller in the bottom, as her life went on. Watching my momma progress into dementia was much like going through a tunnel, cuz you can't really see whole parts of life going by—you lose perspective; whole scenes are lost behind the walls of the tunnel. Yet the direction is still forward, only because of linear time.

I think my mom went down many side tunnels along the way— places I couldn't see nor understand. At first her side tunnels were terrifying to both of us. I tried to talk her back out of some side tunnel—like "mom, there really is not a man named Miguel who comes and visits you and terrorizes you at night". But what did I know? Then, when the male visitor was nice and was her boyfriend who would come and take her places I just loved to hear about that side tunnel.

Then, she was outside in the rain looking for the train; the tunnel to the train to visit her daughter. Then she was on the dance floor at the Accordion Festival dancing to Spanish Eyes with me— her song with my father—did she think she was in a tunnel of love again with him?

"You are my sunshine" we would just start to sing and she would come out of a blind tunnel real quick and be right there singing with us in the bright sunny tunnel instead. That was a sweet one.

I hope your tunnel was real bright at the end momma, and hope it still is now on the other side, and the end of the funnel/tunnel opened out to lots of bright sunshine!

10/20/2020

Word: Visceral – intuitive, that which affects the viscera

Defined in Merriam Webster:
1. Felt in or as if in the internal organs of the body: DEEP
2. Not intellectual: INSTINCTIVE, UNREASONING
3. Dealing with crude or elemental emotions: EARTHY
4. Of, relating to, or located on or among the viscera: SPLANCHNIC

Poem: Selection from "Sweetness" by Stephen Dunn
"…Often a sweetness comes
as if on loan, stays just long enough
to make sense of what it means to be alive,…"

Meal: Indian food take out (distanced meals in backyard); Rice pudding, Carrot and Lavender cupcakes

Prompt: Write about an experience you had with sweetness
By Maria

It was a busy evening on the med-surg floor that evening. I had 4 or 5 patients, had to cover IV meds for a LVN and one of my patients was dying. He and his wife were collateral damage from the fire in their home. She was so badly burned she was taken to a burn unit in another city. He, my patient, had a trach and oxygen and dyspnea and an oxygen saturation level that would not cooperate. When I started my evening shift I was surprised to see he was still alive. Last week, at the end of my shift I said goodbye to him. I would be off for two days and didn't expect him to live that long.

He looked pale, weaker but he managed a smile when I entered his room. We talked as I held his hand. Touch, warmth, communicating something beyond words. My nursing assessment was done in our hands. I sat there. He'd open and close his eyes. They belied his strong grip. I hear my name on the intercom and need to leave him. I tell him I'll be right back.

Apparently, my sweet little old lady who was practically strapped to her bed was Houdini and walking up and down the halls nude. Just in time to see her doctor! Yikes!! I see her doctor walking towards me. He mumbles some doctorish complaint. I fire back my workload and mention my dying patient. He shuts up and leaves me alone. I help the beauty queen back to her room. We laugh and she promises to stay put and keep her clothes on. I leave and quickly check on my other patients then return to see my friend.

He miraculously summons energy and begins to talk to me about his wife. Their home, their life together. How she is in another hospital. How he wants her to know that he loves her. He needs to tell her. She needs to know. Can I do that for him. Can I get her on the phone? She must know!

I have no idea how, but I find the correct hospital, the correct floor and the correct nurse. His wife is unavailable, and my friend is too weak to talk. He listens as I speak for him, eyes open and attentive. His wife's nurse promises to tell her that he called to tell her how much he loved her. Message delivered. We are both relieved. I hold his hand and now it's time for 1800 meds. I tell him I'll be back. He doesn't want to let go of my hand. I squeeze hard and force a quiet smile.

I quickly and safely administer my 1800 meds and the IVs for the LVN. I am grateful all my patients receive the correct medication.

I rush back to his room. He looks much weaker, respirations shallow, irregular, eyes closed more than open. I sit down and hold his hand. His grip tightens. I talk to him. Tell him I'm here. I'm with him…. Until I hear my name on the intercom again. I tell him I'll be right back. Another family member has a question for me. I respond quickly and go back to my friend's room.

The next couple of hours is spent like that. Sitting and holding his hand in this sacred space, then leaving briefly to attend to my other patients. Nurses see my dilemma. They know and help when they can but sometimes it is only I who has the answer.

Each time I return to my friend, he shifts to the next level. I remind him, he's not alone. The last time I leave I know it won't take long. I promise him I'll be back in less than 3 minutes. I know it won't take long. He lets go of my hand and I rush all the way down the long hallway, answer the question and return. I hold his hand and squeeze. He doesn't squeeze back. His hand is warm, his face relaxed. He had been Cheyne stoking and I think the pause is exceptionally long. I wait and talk to comfort him and remind him his wife feels his love. The pause becomes constant.

He is no longer breathing. I wonder if I let him down. Did he die alone? Was he alive and just too weak to squeeze my hand? He was afraid of dying alone. In that 2-minute span he left. I think back now and wonder if I could have done more.

I step outside and cry. A nurse is looking for me AGAIN! I tell her I need a few minutes. She sees my anguish and tells me she'll deal with it. Not to worry. Bittersweet.

06/20/17

Word: Vulnerability

Defined in Merriam Webster:
1. Capable of being physically or emotionally wounded
2. Open to attack or damage: ASSAILABLE
3. Liable to increased penalties but entitled to increased bonuses after winning a game in contract bridge

Poem: From "At the Fishhouses" by Elizabeth Bishop (1911-1979)
from "The Complete Poems (Farrar, Straus and Giroux, 1983
"...If you should dip your hand in,
your wrist would ache immediately,
your bones would begin to ache and your hand would burn
as if the water were a transmutation of fire
that feeds on stones and burns with a dark gray flame.
If you tasted it, it would first taste bitter,
then briny, then surely burn your tongue.
It is like what we imagine knowledge to be:
dark, salt, clear, moving, utterly free,
drawn from the cold hard mouth
of the world, derived from the rocky breasts
forever, flowing and drawn, and since
our knowledge is historical, flowing, and flown."

Meal: Polenta, chickpea salad, green salad, nectarine salad, two sorbets

Prompt: Write about a time you dipped your hand into the fire
By Mary

I was 41, with an "around the world" ticket after putting my work/ home on hold. I had been one of the AIDS warriors for many years; my spark was fading. The house is so quiet as my creative and phenomenal daughter is off at college.

I was flying into Katmandu from India. Feeling expectant, excited and tapped out. I already had GI problems, sleepless nights and I'm only 2 weeks into my 6-month adventure. As the plane comes toward Katmandu, the wind picks up. The small plane is shaking and bouncing. The woman next to me is hyperventilating. I have my arm around her, trying to calm her even though my heart is also beyond tachycardic. I thought "If I die today, how long before my family finds out?" Damn, I should have listened to my friend JoJo "You can watch the travel channel- you don't have to go there".

It was 20 minutes of high anxiety when the clouds parted. There was a breath takingly beautiful city surrounded by the most majestic mountains. Seeing where we were going offered no real assurance that we'd actually get there but I now felt certain that I was right in coming. My soul so yearned for something that was here.

Fast forward 2 months: I feel I did jump into the flame of Nepal. I trekked with amazing people from all over the world through lush and harsh country, humble villages. I worked on a mobile clinic helping with medical issues I had only read about in the past. I spent 10 days at a Buddhist temple where I only spoke 50-100 words per day, a lifetime record for me. I had a fascinating co-traveler who I would have never known in my life at home. I stayed another month to explore Nepal. I fell in love with many people, children and places. But, mostly, I fell in love with myself. I delighted myself almost every day with little and big acts of courage and wonder; laughed a lot trying to communicate with others, pushed my body more that I had so far in this life and totally, totally savored simple things- like SNEEKERs (Snickers) Bars when I could find one. I cleared the way to step into the deep well of awe. I left with a reinforced sense of trust in myself and the universe.

It felt like the life there, for me, was a transmutation of fire into a greater relationship with myself.

07/16/2019

Word: Weave

Defined in Merriam Webster:
1. To interlace especially to form a texture, fabric, or design
2. To direct (something, such as a body) in a winding or zigzag course especially to avoid obstacles
   (a) to form (cloth) by interlacing strands (as of yarn)
   (b) to interlace (threads) into cloth
   (c) to make (something, such as a basket) by interweaving
3. (a) to produce by elaborately combining elements: CONTRIVE
   (b) to unite in a coherent whole
   (c) to introduce as an appropriate element: work in usually used with in or into

Poem: Selection from "Wait "by Galway Kinnell
"…Only wait a while and listen.
Music of hair,
Music of pain,
music of looms weaving all our loves again.
Be there to hear it, it will be the only time,
most of all to hear your whole existence,…"

Meal: Cheesy Grits with greens, strawberry salad, fruit; Chocolate Almonds, Godiva chocolate, Lemon thins
Cheesy Grits with Greens Recipe:
4 slices of tofu bacon, chopped
1 onion, chopped
2 cups vegetable stock

2 cups whole milk or plant-based milk

Kasher salt and freshly ground black pepper

1 cup quick cooking grits

1 cup grated smoked Gouda Cheese

2 tablespoons heavy cream

Butter (can use plant-based butter) to finish

Chopped chives, for garnish

Collard Greens:

1 large bundle collard greens (1 pound), washed well

1 tablespoon olive oil

5 cloves garlic, minced

Kosher salt and freshly ground black pepper

¼ cup vegetable stock

INSTRUCTIONS:

Grits:

In a medium sized saucepan over medium heat add 1 tablespoon virgin olive oil and then add tofu bacon strips. Stir with a wooden spoon. Add the onion and sauté until tender about 3-5 minutes

Add the vegetable stock, milk, and salt and pepper to taste and bring to a boil.

Once boiling, gradually add the grits in a low steady stream, whisking continually. Reduce the heat to low and stir frequently un the liquid is almost absorbed, and grits are thick, about 10 minutes.

Add the Gouda cheese, whisking all the while to melt the cheese. Stir in heavy cream and butter. Taste for seasoning and add salt and pepper if needed. Sprinkle with chives and serve immediately with the Collard Greens.

Collard Greens:
Remove and discard the tough stems and center ribs of the collard greens. Stack the leaves and roll tightly into a cylinder. Thinly slice the collards into ribbons about 1/16th of an inch thick. Repeat with any remaining collard greens.

Heat a large skillet over medium heat and add 1 tablespoon olive oil. She the oil shimmers add the garlic and sauté for 30 seconds. Add the collard greens, toss quickly with tongs, and sauté until bright green, about 3-4 minutes. Season with salt and pepper to taste. Stir in the vegetable stock and cook until the liquid evaporates, another 2 minutes. Serve immediately with the grits.

Prompt: A time when I was a weaver….
By Penny

I am now learning to "weave". The technic is to weave not yarn but emotions, memories, perspectives, that have become separate from the whole of who I am today. A feeling, emotion, images of pain, anger, betrayal, wrong doings, that have become a frayed separateness of my loving heart—something to disassociate from, to not own as my doing, my being.

The technic of "weaving" is to reclaim these strands of fragmented feelings, emotions, pains, angers, and bring them back into my loving heart. To accept that they are mine. To reclaim them from my analytic brain that has judged them, cursed them as somehow as not part of my being. That these emotions and feelings somehow have more power over my loving heart or is a conflict to it, to who I perceive I am.

I am taking each feeling from the major and minor trauma memories of my own mind, holding them lovingly in one hand and in the other hand I hold total acceptance, unconditional love and exam unjudgmentally these feelings, these memories, betrayals, pains, and as though through a magical alchemy, a new fabric is produced. A new weave, an integration. A mending occurs. Through imagery and this practice of experiencing dissonant aspects of myself, I am learning my patterns of emotion, reclaiming, and embracing all of myself.

12/10/2019

Word: WONDER

Defined in Merriam Webster:
1. Something or someone that is very surprising, beautiful, amazing, etc.
2. A feeling caused by seeing something that is very surprising or hard to believe
3. The quality of exciting, amazed admiration
   (a) rapt attention or astonishment at something awesomely mysterious or new to one's experience
   (b) a feeling of doubt or uncertainty

Poem: "A Pause" by James Richardson (born 1950)

Meal: Happy Soup (Udon with vegetables), Roasted Salmon, Bread; Chocolate cake

Prompt: (Not archived)
By Maria

Feelings, how am I feeling?
I wonder
I didn't really know as a child
It took forever and a day to unwrap those feelings
to unmask them
they wiggled and squiggled
they turned into unrecognizable blobs when I was a child
I knew how you were feeling
I could easily gather that information and recite it for you

But if you asked how I felt, I wouldn't know what to say

You never asked

I wonder

Why not?

This child never had the chance to wonder,

She wondered why it happened to her

Darkness stopped her wondering

Pain made her numb, she dare not look inside

Oh, to be able to wonder

To have the freedom to wonder

The safety to explore

I like wonder

The indecision

The multitude of possibilities

The vague commitment

A romantic and sentimental connotation

An opening of doors

So many possibilities

So much yet unanswered

I wonder who is calling and what they have to say

I wonder what I'll be when I grow up

I wonder what I'm getting for Christmas

I wonder what I'll wear to work tomorrow

I wonder if I'll be at the same job next year

All uncertainties

No clear landing

Like my once undiscovered feelings

Finally,

One day the dam breaks!!!!

Was it one day?

Or over the course of many years?

Da igual

Those feelings were freed!!

With that came my freedom to

WONDER

Chapter 4

Starting A Writing Medicine Group

There are numerous types of writing groups one can join or start. A Writing Medicine Group, like the one shared in this book, has some group norms and objectives from the start. The objectives are to have a forum for expression that is free from judgement and criticism, a space to be heard and witnessed, and to build greater self-awareness and resilience as Caregivers/ Care providers. The group norms are to be non-judgmental or critical of other's writings, to be fully present to the group and be an active listener, and to fully respect personal boundaries. We do not ask the writer for more details or explanations regarding what they choose to share in their writing.

Rules for the group have to do with confidentiality. What is shared in the group, stays in the group. Group members are free to decline to share a writing without having to explain why. Respect towards others always demonstrated.

A group leader or point person is helpful. Often a leader will emerge, if not stated at the onset. Jenny has been our leader/ point person from the start. We agree on the word each month for the next month and Jenny will take it from there. We have appreciated her skill with bringing words, poems, and prompts for us to write on over the years. None of us have felt like this dynamic should change.

Structure for a group organizer could be having each member take a turn at organizing the monthly group. The group organizer could be elected through a democratic vote by group members. There are many other ways a group organizer may emerge. A group organizer is strongly recommended for a successful ongoing group.

Our group is comprised of women, all women working in medicine as care providers. We did not start out with the idea that it would consist only of women. We opened the invitation to our colleagues working in the Community Health Clinics and it is the women that responded with interest.

Many of our colleagues that came a time or two decided it was not useful for them. This concept of group writing isn't for everyone and the group has a lot of freedom for our colleagues that may want to come and see what the group is about without having any pressure to feel they must commit to participating ongoing. Some of our colleagues have come for periods of time and then circumstances in life change, and participation stops. This is to be expected and they know they are always welcome to return. No one has every left the writing group feeling they were not welcome to participate.

Qualities and characteristics for a successful writing group participant has to do with a person's ego strengths and respect for personal boundaries. In a Writing Medicine Group, it is not unusual for a participant to share some personal experience and feelings through their writings. Individuals that participate need to have awareness of their personal boundaries and be able to take responsibility for how much to reveal to others without being left feeling vulnerable or wounded through disclosing. The group is not a therapy group and if a member appears to need therapy there is no harm in speaking with this member on a one-to-one bases to compassionately encourage this work be done. The group should never try to take on a role it is not equipped for.

The Writing Medicine Group is for the individual's personal journey to greater self-awareness. Self-awareness is an essential aspect for good mental health in any profession and especially needed in professions that are caring to the needs of others. If as a care provider/caregiver, we are not aware of where our personal wounds are, if we are not aware of what trigger's our limbic brain (fight or flight responses), we will not be able to respond to situations with others that require a controlled, calming presence to aide others. Resilience comes from a place of self-knowing and self-care. Every time a personal wound gets opened or revealed, there is a need for healing by acknowledging the wound's existence and giving it care. This does not mean we are to disengage in what we are doing in the present when we feel the wound reopen, it means that after we have attended to what is in the moment we will not forget the wound is there and will take some time to revisit it. It still needs more healing, perhaps at a deeper level now.

It takes a tremendous amount of energy to wall off our own wounds to attend to the needs of others. The term "compassion fatigue" comes from the caregiver's desire to tend to the needs of others while having not cared for their own needs. When the intellectual brain is fighting with the limbic brain it takes its toll by depleting one's energy to continue to be present to the needs of those we signed up to care for.

The other way "compassion fatigue" develops is institutional. When the work setting is not sensitive to workers need for self-care and self-care is not acknowledged, not provided, or promoted within the workday. When this occurs day after day, the result will be worker "burn out".

Through the group writing experiences more of ourselves is being revealed and organized in ways that may have escaped our conscious insight in the past. In sharing our writings, our personal stories and our life assumptions, the mirror of our reality is expanded. We are allowing for a greater depth of experience by revealing more of ourselves with this group Writing Medicine medium. Writing is good medicine.

Printed in the United States
by Baker & Taylor Publisher Services